# Journal of Biblical and Theological Studies

### EDITORS

**Managing Editor:** Daniel S. Diffey (Grand Canyon University)
**Associate Editor:** Ryan A. Brandt (Grand Canyon University)

### BOOK REVIEW EDITORS

**Biblical Studies:** Paul Cable (Mid-America Reformed Seminary)
**Church History and Historical Theology:** Chad Brand (Oklahoma Baptist University)
**Systematic and Philosophical Theology:** Joshua Farris (Houston Baptist University)
**Philosophy and Ethics:** Danny McDonald (Ancient Christian Studies and Boyce College)
**Ministry and Pastoral Theology:** Justin McLendon (Grand Canyon University)

### PRODUCTION AND DESIGN

**Production Editor:** Dawn Juhas
**Production Editor:** Lauren Krueger
**Graphic Designer:** Diana Cheek
**Graphic Designer:** Billie Worth

Copyright © 2016 Grand Canyon University College of Theology. All rights reserved. Except for brief quotations in critical publications or reviews, no part of this book may be reproduced in any manner without prior written permission from the publisher. Write: Permissions, Wipf and Stock Publishers, 199 W. 8th Ave., Suite 3, Eugene, OR 97401.

Pickwick Publications
An Imprint of Wipf and Stock Publishers
199 W. 8th Ave., Suite 3
Eugene, OR 97401

www.wipfandstock.com

PAPERBACK ISBN: 978-1-5326-0436-2

Manufactured in the U.S.A.

# *Editorial Note*

## Ryan A. Brandt and Daniel S. Diffey

## AN INTRODUCTION TO JBTS

We are pleased to introduce you to the Journal of Biblical and Theological Studies (JBTS). Each year we will publish two issues of this journal that will be made available both in print and online. At times, like this issue, we will have a special focus.

JBTS attempts to accomplish two primary purposes. First, the journal seeks a broader audience within evangelicalism, attempting to fill a particular void in the evangelical literature. While there are plenty of evangelical journals that cater to specific denominational or theological concerns, there are few that serve the evangelical world at large. JBTS is an original journal that caters to the broader evangelical spectrum.

Second, the journal seeks the audience of both scholars and students alike. Academic journals are often written by scholars for other scholars. They are technical in nature, assuming a robust knowledge of the field. There are fewer journals that seek to introduce biblical and theological scholarship that is also accessible to students in these fields. JBTS seeks to bridge the existing gap by providing high-level scholarship and research to both scholars and students. It thus seeks to create original scholarship that is readable and accessible. In doing this we also want to introduce what good research and scholarship look like to our students.

Our first issue is focused on Pauline studies and features five articles. The contributors of this issue range in their denominational and theological perspectives, which is an important part of the vision and mission of this journal. The first article is authored by Aaron O'Kelley and will introduce the reader to some of the key points of discussion within the debate on the New Perspective on Paul, particularly whether Paul's understanding of righteousness should be viewed in terms of ecclesiology or soteriology. The second article, by David Burnette, focuses on the theme of the kingdom of God and how this relates to Paul and his theology. The last three articles should be read together as a conversation. Joshua Greever and John Frederick each provide a detailed review article of Charles Lee Irons' recent monograph on the topic of the righteousness of God. Greever and Frederick represent two different views within Pauline studies: Greever is more sympathetic to the Reformational view of Paul while Frederick is more sympathetic to the New Perspective. Each author provides a detailed discussion of their thoughts and interaction with Irons' argument. Irons then offers a detailed response. The hope is that this conversation will help readers, scholars and students alike, to be able to think through some of these important issues and to engage the scholarly literature better.

# Paul's Doctrine of Justification: Ecclesiology or Soteriology?

## Aaron O'Kelley

Aaron O'Kelley serves as a Pastor at Cornerstone Community Church in Jackson, TN and as Director of the Southern Baptist Theological Seminary, Jackson Extension

**Abstract:** The new perspective on Paul places the doctrine of justification primarily in the category of ecclesiology, as a declaration of covenant membership that is common to Jews and Gentiles alike. However, Paul's use of key terms in the realm of "righteousness" terminology, as well as the phrase "works of the law" indicates that Paul's doctrine of justification belongs in the category of soteriology, referring primarily to the standing of individuals before God. Nevertheless, this traditional Protestant understanding of justification has significant implications for the doctrine of the church, which the new perspective has rightly pointed out.

**Key terms:** new perspective on Paul, justification, righteousness, works of the law, soteriology, ecclesiology.

## Background: The Newness of the New Perspective

In an article appropriately titled for the current climate of Pauline studies, Stephen Westerholm remarks, "Justification by Faith is the Answer: What is the Question?".[1] Since the rise of the so-called "new perspective on Paul" anticipated by Krister Stendahl,[2] pioneered by E. P. Sanders,[3] and developed and promoted by N. T.

---

1. Stephen Westerholm, "Justification by Faith is the Answer: What is the Question?" *Concordia Theological Quarterly* 70 (2006): 197-217.

2. Krister Stendahl, "The Apostle Paul and the Introspective Conscience of the West," *Harvard Theological Review* 56 (1963): 199-215; reproduced in Krister Stendahl, *Paul Among Jews and Gentiles* (Philadelphia: Fortress, 1976), 78-96.

3. E. P. Sanders, *Paul and Palestinian Judaism: A Comparison of Patterns of Religion* (Minneapolis: Fortress, 1977); idem, *Paul, the Law, and the Jewish People* (Philadelphia: Fortress, 1983); idem, *Paul, Past Masters* (New York: Oxford University Press, 1991).

Wright[4] and James D. G. Dunn,[5] that question has become a pressing one. The newness of the new perspective is relative to the mainstream Protestant reading of Paul that prevailed until the late 20th century. Central to the new perspective project is the claim that Protestants have misinterpreted Paul for centuries by abstracting him from his first-century context and forcing out of him answers to questions that he never meant to address. As a result, Paul's doctrine of justification has been distorted into a legal transaction aimed to soothe individual consciences before God rather than a covenantal declaration that binds Jews and Gentiles together in Christ.

While not all new perspective proponents speak with one voice on the issue of justification, they do stand united in an attempt to discard the Lutheran[6] baggage that has accrued to it since the sixteenth century and place the doctrine squarely within the context of Jew-Gentile relations encountered in the Pauline mission. Certainly, all faithful interpreters of Scripture should seek to place Paul in his own context, and the importance of Jew-Gentile relations in Paul's development of the doctrine of justification, especially in the book of Galatians, should not be missed. Insofar as it has drawn attention to a neglected aspect of Protestant doctrinal formulation, the new perspective has done a great service to the church. However, this essay will argue that, to the degree that the new perspective defines justification as an element that belongs primarily under the doctrine of the church (ecclesiology) rather than the doctrine of salvation (soteriology), it distorts Paul's teaching. For Paul, justification is a soteriological doctrine that addresses the standing of individual sinners before God, and it is from this individual, soteriological base that the important ecclesiological ramifications addressed in the Pauline mission emerge. Therefore, the argument will proceed by defining the new perspective's doctrine of justification as ecclesiology, drawing

---

4. N. T. Wright, "The Paul of History and the Apostle of Faith," *Tyndale Bulletin* 29 (1978): 61-88; idem, *The Climax of the Covenant: Christ and the Law in Pauline Theology* (Minneapolis: Fortress, 1991); idem, *What Saint Paul Really Said: Was Paul of Tarsus the Real Founder of Christianity?* (Grand Rapids: Eerdmans, 1997); idem, "Romans and the Theology of Paul," in *Pauline Theology*, vol. 3, *Romans*, ed. David M. Hay and E. Elizabeth Johnson (Atlanta: Society of Biblical Literature, 2002), 30-67; idem, *The Letter to the Romans*, in vol. 10 of *The New Interpreter's Bible*, ed. Leander E. Keck et al. (Nashville: Abingdon, 2002), 393-770; idem, *Paul: In Fresh Perspective* (Minneapolis: Fortress, 2005); idem, "New Perspectives on Paul," in *Justification in Perspective: Historical Developments and Contemporary Challenges*, ed. Bruce L. McCormack (Grand Rapids: Baker Academic, 2006), 243-64; idem, *Justification: God's Plan and Paul's Vision* (Downers Grove, IL: IVP Academic, 2009); idem, *Paul and the Faithfulness of God*, 2 vols. (Minneapolis: Fortress, 2013).

5. James D. G. Dunn, *The New Perspective on Paul: Collected Essays* (Tübingen: Mohr Siebeck, 2005); idem, *Jesus, Paul, and the Law: Studies in Mark and Galatians* (Louisville: Westminster John Knox, 1990); idem, *Romans*, Word Biblical Commentary, vols. 38a-38b (Dallas: Word, 1988); idem, *The Theology of Paul the Apostle* (Grand Rapids: Eerdmans, 1998).

6. The Lutheran tradition is often regarded as the primary example of the "old perspective" on Paul, viewing his doctrine of justification as a legal declaration regarding the standing of individuals before him. However, it is important to note that many Protestants outside the Lutheran tradition—especially in the Reformed tradition—have held to the same view of justification and have read Paul in the same way.

from the proposal of its most prominent voice, N. T. Wright.[7] It will then proceed by critiquing this definition in light of exegetical insights from Paul's letters, and offering an alternative way to integrate ecclesiology into the discussion without distorting the doctrine of justification.

## Justification *as* Ecclesiology: The Claim of the New Perspective

The new perspective on Paul emerged from a new perspective on Second Temple Judaism proposed by E. P. Sanders in his 1977 work, *Paul and Palestinian Judaism*. One of Sanders's stated purposes in this work was "to destroy the view of Rabbinic Judaism which [was at the time] still prevalent in much, perhaps most, New Testament scholarship," namely, the view that Judaism was a legalistic religion where righteousness before God was earned by good works.[8] By contrast, Sanders proposed that the diverse strands of Judaism from the years 200 B.C. to A.D. 200 exhibited a common pattern of religion that was essentially gracious in character, a pattern he termed "covenantal nomism." He described this pattern of religion in eight propositions:

> (1) God has chosen Israel and (2) given the law. The law implies both (3) God's promise to maintain the election and (4) the requirement to obey. (5) God rewards obedience and punishes transgression. (6) The law provides for means of atonement, and atonement results in (7) maintenance or re-establishment of the covenantal relationship. (8) All those who are maintained in the covenant by obedience, atonement and God's mercy belong to the group which will be saved. An important interpretation of the first and last points is that election and ultimately salvation are considered to be by God's mercy rather than human achievement.[9]

---

7. It is impossible in the scope of this essay to investigate in detail the views of other scholars, but an ecclesiological focus can be discerned in both James D. G. Dunn and Richard B. Hays as well. See Dunn, "The New Perspective on Paul"; Richard B. Hays, "Justification," in *The Anchor Bible Dictionary*, vol. 3, *H-J*, ed. David Noel Freedman (New York: Doubleday, 1992), 1129-33. Dunn's more recent work, however, indicates that he may be seeking a rapprochement between the ecclesiological emphasis of the new perspective and the soteriological emphasis of traditional Protestant theology. See James D. G. Dunn, "The Justice of God: A Renewed Perspective on Justification by Faith," in *The New Perspective on Paul: Collected Essays* (Tübingen: Mohr Siebeck, 2005), 187-205 [originally published in *JTS* 43 (1992): 1-22]; idem, "Paul and Justification by Faith," in *The New Perspective on Paul: Collected Essays* (Tübingen: Mohr Siebeck, 2005), 361-74 [originally published in *The Road from Damascus: The Impact of Paul's Conversion on His Life, Thought, and Ministry*, ed. R. N. Longenecker (Grand Rapids: Eerdmans, 1997), 85-101]; idem, "Philippians 3.2-14 and the New Perspective on Paul," in *The New Perspective on Paul: Collected Essays* (Tübingen: Mohr Siebeck, 2005), 463-84; idem, "The New Perspective: Whence, What, and Wither?" in *The New Perspective on Paul: Collected Essays* (Tübingen: Mohr Siebeck, 2005), 1-88; idem, *The Theology of Paul the Apostle*, 334-89.

8. Sanders, *Paul and Palestinian Judaism*, xii.

9. Ibid., 422.

For Sanders and his followers, this new light from Paul's Jewish context demands a new approach to the Pauline writings, for Paul can no longer be read as the apostle of grace who fought off a (non-existent) Jewish legalism. Instead, his polemic must be reinterpreted, and along with it his doctrine of justification.

Dunn and Wright have accepted the basic contours of Sanders's approach to Second Temple Judaism, but both have found Sanders's work on Paul inadequate.[10] While they agree with Sanders that Paul's polemic is not aimed at legalism, they have moved beyond Sanders by proposing a new target for Paul: Jewish nationalism. According to Dunn and Wright, Paul's polemic takes on Second Temple Judaism for its boast in national privilege to the exclusion of the Gentiles. The Pauline phrase "works of the law" does not refer to Jewish attempts to earn favor with God through good works. Rather, it focuses primarily on Jewish boundary markers, badges that divide Jews from Gentiles, most notably circumcision, Sabbath, and food laws.[11] And since Paul's doctrine of justification by faith stands opposed to justification by works of the law, they argue that justification addresses primarily the issue of Jew-Gentile relations.

Because Wright has been most explicit in defining justification by faith as an ecclesiological doctrine, this study will focus entirely on his proposal.[12] His argument stems from his understanding of righteousness as covenantal in nature. The key Pauline phrase "the righteousness of God" (Rom 1:17; 3:21, 25-26; 10:3; 2 Cor 5:21) refers, according to Wright, to God's faithfulness to his covenant with Israel.[13] Given this basic understanding of righteousness terminology, Wright unfolds his doctrine of justification primarily in covenantal terms. He argues that justification is God's declaration that one is in the covenant, and that faith is the identifying mark (i.e., a badge) by which God makes this declaration. For example, the righteousness of the law that Paul rejected in Philippians 3:9 "is not a moralistic or self-help righteousness, but the

---

10. James D. G. Dunn, "The New Perspective on Paul," in *The New Perspective on Paul: Collected Essays* (Tübingen, 2005), 89-95; Wright, "The Paul of History," 81-84.

11. Dunn, "The New Perspective on Paul," 98-101; Wright, *Romans*, 460-61.

12. Of course, my argument does not assert that all new perspective proponents stand in agreement with Wright on everything. In fact, there are numerous differences between them. Nevertheless, because every study must have limits, this response to the new perspective will focus on N. T. Wright and assume that where Wright's views overlap with those of others, the argument of this paper will also be pertinent to them. Where other new perspective proponents may depart from Wright is outside the scope of this study. I believe this approach is justified because there is widespread agreement that what constitutes the "new perspective" is a new way of viewing Paul's polemic, which in turn results in a new way of interpreting his doctrine of justification. All proponents of the new perspective, to one degree or another, share this hermeneutical and theological paradigm shift.

13. Wright, *What Saint Paul Really Said*, 95-111; idem, *Paul and the Faithfulness of God*, 2:795-804; see also Wright's unprecedented interpretation of 2 Corinthians 5:21 in idem, "On Becoming the Righteousness of God: 2 Corinthians 5:21," in *Pauline Theology*, vol. 2, *1 & 2 Corinthians*, ed. David M. Hay (Minneapolis: Fortress, 1993), 200-08. On the righteousness of God as his covenant faithfulness see also Dunn, *The Theology of Paul the Apostle*, 340-46; Richard B. Hays, "Justification," in *The Anchor Bible Dictionary*, vol. 3, *H-J*, ed. David Noel Freedman (New York: Doubleday, 1992), 1129-33.

status of orthodox Jewish covenant membership."[14] By contrast, Paul desired "a righteousness from God," which Wright defines as "the status of covenant *membership*; it is the gift of God, not something acquired in any way by the human beings involved; and this gift is bestowed on faith."[15] Instead of relying on the badge of circumcision to define his covenant membership, Paul recognized faith as the badge that identifies God's true covenant people, a badge accessible to Gentiles without requiring them to convert to Judaism.

Crucial to Wright's doctrine is the non-initiatory nature of justification. In other words, for Wright, justification is not about becoming a Christian but about marking out those who are already Christians. By demarcating members of the covenant in his justifying declaration, God does not change anyone's status; rather, he recognizes who already belongs to him:

> Justification in this setting, then, is not a matter of *how someone enters the community of the true people of God*, but of *how you tell who belongs to that community*, not least in the period of time before the eschatological event itself, when the matter will become public knowledge . . . 'Justification' in the first century was not about how someone might establish a relationship with God. It was about God's eschatological definition, both future and present, of who was, in fact, a member of his people. In Sanders's terms, it was not so much about 'getting in', or indeed about 'staying in,' as about 'how you could tell who was in'. In standard Christian theological language, it wasn't so much about soteriology as about ecclesiology; not so much about salvation as about the church.[16]

Justification by faith is, then, the present anticipation of final justification, when God's covenant people will be vindicated publicly. For Wright, final justification is not based on faith; it is, as Paul affirms in Romans 2:13, by works: "[Justification] occurs in the future, as we have seen on the basis of the entire life a person has led in the power of the Spirit—that is, it occurs on the basis of 'works' in Paul's redefined sense."[17] Jus-

---

14. Wright, *What Saint Paul Really Said*, 124.

15. Ibid., 124-25, emphasis original.

16. Ibid., 119, emphasis original; see also idem, *Paul: In Fresh Perspective* (Minneapolis: Fortress, 2005), 121-22. In "New Perspectives on Paul," 258, he argues, "The word *dikaioō* is, after all, a declarative word, declaring that something is the case, rather than a word for making something happen or changing the way something is." Yet in a later work, Wright appears to contradict himself: "When the judge in the lawcourt justifies someone, he does not give that person his own particular 'righteousness.' He *creates* the status the vindicated defendant now possesses, by an act of declaration, a 'speech-act' in our contemporary jargon" (*Justification*, 69, emphasis original). If this and similar statements in more recent publications (*Justification*, 91, 135; *Paul and the Faithfulness of God*, 2:945-46) indicate that he has changed his mind and now regards the verdict of justification as one that changes a person's status rather than merely recognizing a status he or she already possesses, then it is a most welcome development. Nowhere, however, does Wright say that he has changed his mind, and thus the apparent contradiction remains in his work.

17. Wright, "New Perspectives on Paul," 260.

tification in the present by faith, then, serves the crucial purpose of marking off God's covenant people (including Jews and Gentiles) in anticipation of their eschatological vindication.[18] It offers assurance to those who possess the badge of faith that they belong to the covenant people and that God will complete the work he began in them (Phil 1:6), issuing in their final justification at the last judgment.

Concluding this brief survey, it is important to recognize the steps that have resulted in a new perspective on justification. Years after Stendahl had raised important questions about Protestant interpretations of Paul, Sanders offered a groundbreaking study of the pattern of religion of Second Temple Judaism, arguing that Jews in Paul's day were not legalists but covenantal nomists who believed strongly in the grace of God. This observation suggested that Paul's polemic against Judaism, and especially against "works of the law," had long been misunderstood. Dunn and Wright adopted Sanders's view of Second Temple Judaism and concluded that Paul's polemic was aimed at Jewish nationalism, primarily exemplified in the boundary markers of the Mosaic Law. The old Lutheran paradigm, in which Paul's writings addressed questions about individual standing before God, had to be discarded. For new perspective proponents, then, the doctrine of justification must be understood in terms of covenant membership, not primarily in terms of guilt and its removal. If justification by faith is the answer, the new perspective proposes that the question is something like this: "How can we know who belongs to the people of God?" Or, perhaps more specifically, "How can Jews and Gentiles be united as the one people of God?" Justification has become primarily a doctrine about the makeup of the church.

## Justification *and* Ecclesiology:
## A Response to the New Perspective

It is impossible to deny that Paul's doctrine of justification has important implications for ecclesiology, particularly in light of the importance of Jew-Gentile relations in the Pauline corpus. However, the new perspective wrongly reduces justification to a declaration of covenant membership, bypassing the important soteriological categories that define the nature of justification in Paul.[19] Reacting to the Lutheran tradition, new perspective arguments appear to ride on a pendulum that has swung too far, minimizing concerns about the salvation of individuals and collapsing ecclesiology into justification. In what follows, it will be demonstrated that for Paul, justification by faith is a soteriological doctrine by which individual sinners are given a new status

18. Wright, *Justification*, 133-36, 251.

19. Gathercole agrees: ". . . one of the problems with a number of New Perspective accounts of justification is that too much importance is frequently attributed to the function of justification as an ecclesiological doctrine, such that its fundamentally soteriological structure is relegated to secondary significance." Simon J. Gathercole, "The Doctrine of Justification in Paul and Beyond: Some Proposals," in *Justification in Perspective: Historical Developments and Contemporary Challenges*, ed. Bruce L. McCormack (Grand Rapids: Baker, 2006), 232.

before God, namely, a status of righteousness, on the basis of Christ's atoning work and through the instrument of faith. Then, on the basis of this justifying verdict that puts sinners in the right before God, the new covenant community is formed without reference to human distinctions, whether ethnic or moral. The argument will proceed by addressing two important terms in the debate, along the way offering observations on important Pauline passages. It will then conclude with an exposition of the ecclesiological implications of the traditional Protestant doctrine of justification.

## Terminology

Crucial to the new perspective doctrine of justification outlined above are the terms "righteousness" and "works of the law." The former has been redefined by the new perspective in terms of covenant membership, and the latter in terms of distinctive Jewish boundary markers. Redefining these terms in such a way leads to redefinition of the phrase "justification by faith." God justifies—that is, recognizes as covenant members—those who have faith (the new covenant identity marker) rather than merely those who are of the "works of the law" (the old covenant identity markers). However, these redefinitions do not fit the biblical evidence, as will be demonstrated below.

**Righteousness.**[20] Is it true, as Wright claims, that "'Righteousness,' when applied to humans, is, at bottom, the status of being a member of the covenant."?[21] If so, then one must ask why it does not have the same significance when applied to God. New perspective proponents have argued unequivocally that "the righteousness of God" is his faithfulness to the covenant (not his membership in the covenant), so that God is righteous when he fulfills the obligations that he took upon himself by entering into covenant with Israel.[22] The shortcomings of this definition of God's righteousness will not be pursued here.[23] For now, it will suffice to acknowledge that covenant faithfulness is at least one aspect of God's righteousness. In any case, taking the new perspective argument on its own terms, one would expect some kind of explanation for the clear equivocation that occurs when "righteousness" is applied to God and when it is applied to humans. For the new perspective, to say that God is righteous is to say that he has fulfilled every covenant obligation, but the same connotation does not seem

---

20. Of course, it is important to keep in mind throughout this discussion that justification belongs in the category of righteousness terminology, as both the Hebrew root צדק and the Greek root δικ- demonstrate. Unfortunately, this semantic relationship has been obscured in English.

21. Wright, *Romans*, 491; see also idem, *The Climax of the Covenant*, 214.

22. Wright, *What Saint Paul Really Said*, 95-111; idem, *Romans*, 403-06; Dunn, *The Theology of Paul the Apostle*, 340-46; Hays, "Justification," 1129-32.

23. See Mark A. Seifrid, "Righteousness Language in the Hebrew Scriptures and Early Judaism," in *Justification and Variegated Nomism*, vol. 1, *The Complexities of Second Temple Judaism*, ed. D. A. Carson, Peter T. O'Brien, and Mark A. Seifrid (Grand Rapids: Baker Academic, 2001), 415-42; Stephen Westerholm, *Perspectives Old and New on Paul: The "Lutheran" Paul and His Critics* (Grand Rapids: Eerdmans, 2004), 284-86.

to be present when applied to human beings. A human being's righteousness consists merely in his or her covenant membership. As the long and tortured history of Israel's disobedience demonstrates, covenant membership does not always entail righteousness. In fact, Moses rebuked Israel by saying, "Know, therefore, that the LORD your God is not giving you this good land to possess because of your righteousness, for you are a stubborn people" (Deut 9:6).[24] It is obvious (even in the immediate context, vv. 7ff.) that Moses did not deny that they were true members of the covenant. He rebuked them for being unfaithful to the covenant. Israel was an *un*righteous covenant member, which would apparently be oxymoronic for the new perspective.

One could respond by appealing to the redemptive-historical shift that has occurred in Christ, arguing that in this new age the work of the Son and of the Spirit creates a new covenant people that fulfills what Israel anticipated, such that all who are new covenant members are, in fact, faithful to the covenant obligations and are, therefore, righteous.[25] However, this correct biblical observation does not in any way mitigate equivocation on the term "righteousness." To say that all members of the new covenant are righteous does not entail that righteousness equals covenant membership, anymore than saying that all country club members are wealthy entails that wealth equals country club membership. The mere observation that two terms ("righteous" and "covenant member") apply to the same group in the new covenant era does not justify collapsing their meanings together.[26] New perspective proponents have yet to provide a satisfactory explanation for their equivocation on righteousness terminology.

As mentioned before, "covenant faithfulness" does not exhaust the meaning of righteousness, but it certainly comes closer than "covenant membership." If new perspective proponents consistently interpreted "righteousness" as "covenant faithfulness," no matter to whom it was applied, then their doctrine of justification would improve overnight, as Gathercole observes: "The cash value of this for the interpretation of Paul is that when he speaks of the reckoning of righteousness, it is not just that Christians stand before God as members of the covenant but, rather, that *it is as if they have done everything that God requires.*"[27] If, then, one proceeds to explain this reckoning of the fulfillment of covenant obligations on the basis of Christ's obedience and atoning death, one has entered the territory of traditional Protestant soteriology.

---

24. Unless otherwise indicated, all Scripture quotations are taken from the English Standard Version.

25. Indeed, as a Baptist I would applaud this move!

26. Westerholm [*Perspectives Old and New on Paul*, 291], makes the same point: "Here [in the eyes of some Jews], to be sure, the categories of 'sinners' and 'outsiders' on the one hand and 'righteous' and 'faithful members of the covenant' on the other *overlap* entirely; yet the terms (like 'Cretan' and 'liar') do not *mean* the same thing. If 'sinner' *meant* 'oustider to the covenant,' then human sinfulness would have originated, not with the disobedience of Adam, but with the divine granting of the covenant to Abraham. To the best of my knowledge, evidence of such a notion is not forthcoming."

27. Gathercole, "The Doctrine of Justification in Paul and Beyond," 237, emphasis original.

The preceding argument only exposes an inconsistency within the new perspective. It is now necessary to present a positive case from Paul's own usage of righteousness terminology, a case that will proceed in three steps. First, the primarily ethical meaning of righteousness terminology in Paul must be noted.[28] The main point here is that Paul uses "righteousness" and related terms to refer either to the fulfillment of ethical obligations or to the status one has as a result of fulfilling those ethical obligations. In this sense, a righteous person is defined as one who has done what one ought to do, not as one who is in the covenant. A number of passages make this point forcefully by defining righteousness in opposition to negative terms that are clearly ethical in nature. The string of Old Testament quotations in Romans 3:10-18 begins with the assertion, "None is righteous, no, not one," and this claim is explicated in terms of sinful speech, sinful actions, and a sinful disposition toward God.[29] In Romans 5:7-8 Paul contrasts "a righteous person" for whom one would scarcely die with "sinners" for whom Christ did die, virtually defining righteousness as that which is opposed to sin.[30] In Romans 6:20 the same contrast appears, for Paul writes, "When you were slaves of sin, you were free in regard to righteousness." In 2 Corinthians 6:14-16 he identifies pairs of opposites (light/darkness, Christ/Belial, believer/unbeliever, temple of God/idols), the first of which opposes "righteousness" to "lawlessness." In 1 Timothy 1:9 he contrasts "the just" with "the lawless and disobedient," "the ungodly and sinners," "the unholy and profane," and then he identifies such people as those who violate, in various ways, the second table of the law (vv. 9-11). In 2 Timothy 2:22

---

28. Westerholm [*Perspectives Old and New on Paul*, 263-73] refers to righteousness in this sense as "ordinary dikaiosness."

29. Significantly, the word "righteous" does not appear in either Psalm 14 or Psalm 53, from which Paul quotes in verse 10. This indicates that Paul, quoting loosely from the text, felt that the phrase "None is righteous" expressed the same truth as "no one does good," implying that one who does good is righteous.

30. It makes little difference how one sees "a good person" in verse 7 in relation to "a righteous person," for it would not affect the basic contrast between "a righteous person" and "sinners." However, the argument here presented tightens up slightly when it is recognized that the words "righteous" and "good" are being used synonymously. Paul draws no contrast between "a righteous person" and "a good person" but rather considers them to be the same. See John Murray, *The Epistle to the Romans*, vol. 1 (Grand Rapids: Eerdmans, 1997), 167-68. For an alternative view that distinguishes between "a righteous person" and "a good person," see Wright, *Romans*, 518-19; Thomas R. Schreiner, *Romans*, Baker Exegetical Commentary on the New Testament (Grand Rapids: Baker, 1998), 261-62.

he urges Timothy to "flee youthful passions [that lead to sinful behavior] and [instead] pursue righteousness, faith, love, and peace."[31]

Paul's use of the terms ἀδικία (*adikia*, "unrighteousness") and ἄδικος (*adikos*, "unrighteous") likewise demonstrates that for him righteousness has to do primarily with one's ethical behavior and standing, not one's covenant membership or lack thereof. "Unrighteousness" is paired with "ungodliness" (ἀσέβεια, *asebeia*) in Romans 1:18, and both terms are connected to suppression of the truth about God, leading to creature-worship and its resulting dehumanizing behavior (vv. 18-32).[32] Clearly, in this context God's wrath is directed against people for their sinful rejection of the truth about him, not for their position with respect to the covenant.[33] The "unrighteous" in 1 Corinthians 6:9 are further described as "the sexually immoral," "idolaters," "adulterers," "men who practice homosexuality," "thieves," "the greedy," "drunkards," "revilers," and "swindlers" (vv. 9-10). That these people lack membership in God's new covenant people may be true, but their unrighteousness consists specifically in their attachment to these kinds of sinful behavior. Further examples could be given, but the previous ones demonstrate amply that righteousness terminology in Paul relates primarily to the ethical sphere of meaning, involving the fulfillment (or lack thereof) of one's ethical obligations.[34]

The second step in this argument proceeds to identify the concept of justification in Paul as a legal declaration of righteousness. In its ordinary sense the verb "to justify" (δικαιόω, *dikaioō*) refers to a recognition and legal affirmation that one has

---

31. Throughout this argument it will be presupposed that Paul the apostle wrote all thirteen New Testament letters attributed to him. The most significant of the disputed letters for this study are Ephesians and the Pastoral Epistles. For convincing arguments of their authenticity, see D. A. Carson, Douglas J. Moo, and Leon Morris, *An Introduction to the New Testament* (Grand Rapids: Zondervan, 1992), 305-09, 359-71. Even for those scholars who do not share this presupposition (Dunn denies that Paul wrote any of these letters, and Wright places 1 Timothy and Titus in a non-Pauline category, along with some hesitations about 2 Timothy), these letters should still carry weight in this discussion. Even if Paul did not write them, they certainly stand in the Pauline tradition, and thus one would not expect the use of terminology in these letters to be radically different from Paul or his thought world. Significantly, Dunn argues that the doctrine of justification by grace alone instead of works (in the "Lutheran" sense of these terms) was part of Jewish covenant theology and was presupposed by Paul, though it was later made explicit by the later Pauline epistles (Ephesians and the Pastoral Epistles). Thus, Dunn sees significant continuity between the authentic Pauline epistles and the pseudonymous ones. See James D. G. Dunn, "Whatever Happened to 'Works of the Law'?" in *The New Perspective on Paul: Collected Essays* (Tübingen: Mohr Siebeck, 2005), 387-88.

32. Most commentators argue that "unrighteousness" and "ungodliness" do not describe distinct aspects of rebellion but rather overlap in meaning in Romans 1:18. See C. E. B. Cranfield, *A Critical and Exegetical Commentary on the Epistle to the Romans,* vol. 1, ICC (New York: T & T Clark, 1975), 111-12; James D. G. Dunn, *Romans 1-8,* WBC, vol. 38a (Dallas: Word, 1988), 55-56; Schreiner, *Romans,* 88; contra Murray, 36.

33. Paul also contrasts unrighteousness with the truth in Romans 2:8; 1 Corinthians 13:6; and 2 Thessalonians 2:10, 12.

34. For additional examples see Romans 3:5; 6:13, 16, 18, 19; 10:5; 14:17; 2 Corinthians 9:9-10; 12:13; Ephesians 4:24; 5:9; 6:14; Philippians 3:6; 4:8; Colossians 4:1; 1 Timothy 6:11; 2 Timothy 2:19; 3:16; Titus 1:8; 3:5.

fulfilled his or her ethical obligations.[35] Romans 2:13 reads, "For it is not the hearers of the law who are righteous before God, but the doers of the law who will be justified." Several observations about this verse are noteworthy. First, Paul speaks of justification in the future tense, indicating that he has the final judgment in mind. Second, the parallel structure of the verse indicates clearly that the phrase "righteous before God" and "justified" mean the same thing. Thus, justification for Paul has to do with the legal standing of individuals before God, not primarily with covenant membership. Third, those who will be justified are identified as "the doers of the law" as opposed to the "hearers of the law." Throughout this section (Rom 2:6-16) Paul argues that God's judgment is impartial, so that mere possession of the law provides the Jews with no advantage. What counts before God is what one has done, whether with or without the written law. Justification, therefore, in this context, constitutes a legal declaration that one has fulfilled one's ethical obligations before God, not that one belongs to his covenant people.[36]

First Corinthians 4:4 moves in a similar orbit, for Paul writes, "I am not aware of anything against myself, but I am not thereby acquitted [δεδικαίωμαι, *dedikaiōmai*]. It is the Lord who judges me." Here again, justification is associated with the final judgment and refers to the divine verdict concerning the ethical standing of a person. Quoting from Psalm 51:4 (51:6 in Hebrew and 50:6 LXX) in Romans 3:4, Paul writes of God being justified. Clearly, God does not stand under the authority of a higher court that declares that he has fulfilled his obligations, but this use of the term refers to public vindication, thereby retaining a meaning that is primarily legal in nature (cf. Luke 7:29). God is justified before human beings when he is shown to be just, that is, to have fulfilled his ethical obligations as ruler and judge of creation (Rom 3:25-26). Justification, then, in its normal sense, involves a legal recognition of righteousness. The new perspective's reassignment of the concept to the domain of mere covenant membership finds no support in the use of δικ-terminology in Paul.

The third step in this argument is to point out that justification *by faith* in Paul represents a departure from the ordinary use of the term "justify/justification" and

---

35. The distinction between the ordinary sense of justification and its extraordinary usage in Paul (the latter explained below) is drawn from Westerholm, *Perspectives Old and New on Paul*, 263-85.

36. How Romans 2:13 harmonizes with Paul's doctrine of justification by faith has been debated. Wright ["New Perspectives on Paul," 260] argues that final justification is not by faith but is based on works (in a redefined sense). Schreiner [*Romans*, 119, 144-45] links those who will be justified in 2:13 to the Gentiles mentioned in 2:25-29 and argues that "the doers of the law" are those in whom the Spirit has worked a transformation. However, Murray, 71, offers the best approach to this question: "It is quite unnecessary to find in this verse any doctrine of justification by works in conflict with the teaching of this epistle in later chapters. Whether any will be actually justified by works either in this life or at the final judgment is beside the apostle's interest and design at this juncture. The burden of this verse is that not the hearers or mere possessors of the law will be justified before God but that in terms of the law the criterion is *doing*, not hearing. The apostle's appeal to this principle serves that purpose truly and effectively, and there is no need to import questions that are not relevant to the universe of discourse." See also Westerholm, *Perspectives Old and New on Paul*, 270-71, n. 23, for the same view.

thus constitutes, not a recognition of righteousness, but a declaration of righteousness that changes the legal standing of the one concerning whom it is pronounced. As such, this extraordinary declaration constitutes an initial aspect of salvation that is connected to Christian conversion. Although Paul had previously argued that "the doers of the law will be justified" (Rom 2:13), he makes it clear that no one will belong to this group: "For by works of the law no human being will be justified in his sight" (Rom 3:20; cf. Gal 3:11; 5:4).[37] This dark assessment of the human predicament immediately gives way to the glory of "the righteousness of God through faith in Jesus Christ for all who believe" (Rom 3:22).[38] Although "all have sinned and fall short of the glory of God," both Jews and Gentiles "are justified by his grace *as a gift* through the redemption that is in Christ Jesus" (Rom 3:23-24, emphasis added). It is precisely the gift nature of this justification that makes it extraordinary. Paul likewise speaks of "the gift of righteousness" that is to be received by fallen descendants of Adam in Romans 5:17. Justification in its normal sense refers to a legal declaration that one is or is not righteous, and it is based on whether one has or has not fulfilled one's ethical obligations. But in this extraordinary sense, justification is the verdict of righteousness pronounced over those who have not fulfilled their obligations. Righteousness, then, comes to them as a gift.

Nowhere does Paul spell out this principle more clearly than in Romans 4:1-8, where he enlists Abraham as the example *par excellence* of one who was justified by faith as opposed to works. Crucial to the argument are verses 4-5: "Now to the one who works, his wages are not reckoned according to grace but according to debt, but to the one who does not work but trusts in him who justifies the ungodly, his faith is reckoned for righteousness."[39] Paul labors to spell out clearly the principle that justification by faith is an essentially gracious act of God, as opposed to justification by works, which would involve earning right standing with God, just as a worker earns his wages. The description of God as "him who justifies the ungodly" comes as a shock, not only because it describes Abraham as "ungodly," but primarily because it accuses God of doing what he said he would not do in Exodus 23:7 (cf. Prov 17:15), namely, justify the ungodly. Paul's argument from chapters 1-3 has already established that God's righteousness has been demonstrated through the event of the

---

37. The important phrase "works of the law" will be discussed below.

38. See Wright, *Romans*, 470, and Richard B. Hays, "ΠΙΣΤΙΣ and Pauline Christology: What Is At Stake?" in *Pauline Theology*, vol. 4, *Looking Back, Pressing On*, ed. E. Elizabeth Johnson and David M. Hay (Atlanta: Scholars, 1997), 44-47 for arguments for the subjective genitive interpretation of πιστις Χριστου (*pistis Christou*) in Paul ("the faithfulness of Christ"). This interpretation is ultimately unpersuasive, but even if one adopts it, it only demonstrates that Christ's faithfulness is the basis of our justification. One would then have to look to other passages to see how the believer's faith relates to justification. For arguments against the subjective genitive and for the traditional objective genitive ("faith in Christ"), see Dunn, *Romans 1-8*, 166-67; Moisés Silva, "Faith Versus Works of Law in Galatians," in *Justification and Variegated Nomism*, vol. 2, *The Paradoxes of Paul*, ed. D. A. Carson, Peter T. O'Brien, and Mark A. Seifrid (Grand Rapids: Baker Academic, 2004), 217-48.

39. My translation.

cross (3:25-26), so that his justification of the ungodly does not constitute injustice on his part. Furthermore, Gathercole draws attention to the ways God is described elsewhere in chapter 4: he is the one "who gives life to the dead and calls into existence the things that do not exist" (v. 17) as well as "him who raised from the dead Jesus our Lord" (v. 24).[40] Taken together with the description "him who justifies the ungodly," each phrase indicates that God is the one who, by his declarative acts, creates a new reality. Thus, for God to justify the ungodly is to constitute them as righteous (cf. Rom 5:19), to change their legal standing on the basis of Christ's atoning work. As such, the verdict of justification cannot be a mere recognition of the *status quo* (who is in the covenant, identified by the badge of faith). It must be, rather, a speech act that is declarative in nature, "a declaration by God which, solely because it is uttered, brings about the state of affairs specified by the propositional content."[41] Therefore, it must be an event associated with Christian conversion, the decisive transfer from death to life. Confirmation for this argument may be found in Romans 10:10, where believing unto righteousness and confessing unto salvation are parallel concepts.[42]

Justification by faith, then, constitutes an extraordinary means of gaining righteousness before God, for it bypasses the normal means of doing the law (Rom 2:13) and relies on the grace of God in Christ alone. Does this mean, then, that God lowers his standard and accepts faith as a substitute form of righteousness? Wright repeatedly makes this charge against the traditional Protestant doctrine, but it is a charge that ignores the instrumental (as opposed to meritorious) character of faith.[43] Carson, commenting on Romans 4, explains:

> In Paul's understanding, then, God's imputation of Abraham's faith to Abraham as righteousness *cannot* be grounded in the assumption that faith is itself intrinsically righteous, so that God's "imputing" of it to Abraham is no more than a recognition of what it intrinsically is. If God is counting faith to Abraham *as* righteousness, *he is counting him righteous*—not because Abraham *is* righteous in some inherent way (How can he be? He is ἀσεβής [*asebēs*, "ungodly"]!), but simply because Abraham trusts God and his gracious promise.

---

40. Gathercole, "The Doctrine of Justification in Paul and Beyond," 225-29; idem, "Justified by Faith, Justified by His Blood: The Evidence of Romans 3:21-4:5," in *Justification and Variegated Nomism*, vol. 2, *The Paradoxes of Paul*, ed. D. A. Carson, Peter T. O'Brien, and Mark A. Seifrid (Grand Rapids: Baker Academic, 2004), 165-68.

41. Gregg R. Allison, "Speech Act Theory and Its Implications for the Doctrine of the Inerrancy/Infallibility of Scripture," *Philosophia Christi* 18 (Spring 1995), 8. Allison is not addressing the issue of justification in this quote but is merely explaining the nature of a declarative speech act.

42. Wright ["New Perspectives on Paul," 255-57] argues that "call" belongs to the vocabulary of conversion in Paul, and justification clearly comes after it (Rom 8:30), thereby implying that justification must not be confused with conversion. But see Piper, *The Future of Justification*, 93-98 for an effective response. As Piper argues, justification and conversion are not identical, but "Calling/faith/justification are parts of one event that brings us from God's enmity to his acceptance."

43. Wright, *Romans*, 491; idem, *What Saint Paul Really Said*, 125.

In that sense, then, we are dealing with what systematicians call an alien righteousness.[44]

The fact that Paul can speak of sinners being justified "by faith" (Rom 3:30; 5:1; 9:30; 10:6; Gal 2:16; 3:8, 24; Phil 3:9) as well as "justified in Christ" (Gal 2:17) and "justified by his blood" (Rom 5:9) indicates that the value of faith may be found in its object: Christ crucified. Thus, Paul can speak of Christ as our righteousness (1 Cor 1:30), and he can speak of Christ, who knew no sin, becoming sin for us (by imputation) so that we might become the righteousness of God (by imputation) in him (2 Cor 5:21). Faith itself is not righteousness, but it is counted as righteousness because it connects "the ungodly" to the one in whom they are justified.

Righteousness terminology in Paul moves consistently in the categories of ethical obligation and legal standing, not covenant membership. Justification involves a legal declaration of righteousness, either in the normal sense of recognizing as righteous those who have obeyed the law, or in the extraordinary sense of declaring sinners righteous, sinners who have, by faith, been granted a new standing in Christ.

**Works of the law.** Paul employs the phrase ἔργων νόμου (*ergōn nomou*, "works of the law") six times in his letters: twice to affirm that no one is justified ἐξ ἔργων νόμου (*ex ergōn nomou*, "by works of the law," Rom 3:20; Gal 2:16), once to affirm that one is justified by faith χωρὶς ἔργων νόμου (*chōris ergōn nomou*, "apart from works of the law," Rom 3:28), twice in questions that imply that the Galatians did not receive the Spirit ἐξ ἔργων νόμου (*ex ergōn nomou*, "by works of the law," Gal 3:2, 5), and once to affirm that all who are ἐξ ἔργων νόμου (*ex ergōn nomou*, "of the works of the law") are under a curse (Gal 3:10). In every case faith is mentioned somewhere in the context as the foil to "works of the law." New perspective proponents have seen in these passages dueling identity markers and have argued that what is at stake is the ethnic boundary, or lack thereof, of God's covenant people, with the phrase "works of the law" denoting primarily marks of Jewish identity as opposed to Gentile identity. Paul opposes faith to "works of the law," Jewish boundary markers, not primarily to ground salvation in the grace of God as opposed to human effort expressed through works done in obedience to God, but in order to make his case that Jews and Gentiles alike may be defined as God's covenant people.

However, this interpretation of Paul's language is reductionistic. It drives a wedge between ethnocentrism and legalism, arguing that first-century Jews in Paul's day were guilty of the former but not the latter. Are we to imagine that Jews in the first century saw the identity markers of circumcision, food laws, and Sabbath as badges that marked them out as destitute sinners on the same level, morally speaking, as the Gentiles, except that they had been the recipients of God's electing grace? Or would the badges, to their minds, mark them out as in some sense morally superior and,

---

44. D. A. Carson, "The Vindication of Imputation: On Fields of Discourse and Semantic Fields," in *Justification: What's at Stake in the Current Debates*, ed. Mark Husbands and Daniel J. Treier (Downers Grove: InterVarsity, 2004), 60, emphasis original.

therefore, in a better position before God? Paul's statement to Peter in Galatians 2:15 implies the latter: "We ourselves are Jews by birth and not Gentile sinners." To the typical Jewish mind of the first century, to be a Gentile was to be a "sinner." Of course, this does not mean that Jews understood themselves to be sinless, or even that they did not recognize unfaithful Jews as "sinners" on the same level with the Gentiles.[45] What it does mean, however, is that for them ethnic categories overlapped considerably with moral categories, so that they saw themselves not only as more privileged than Gentiles (in terms of the divine grace they had received), but also as morally superior to them.[46] This kind of ethnocentrism cannot avoid legalism in some sense, for it maintains an anthropocentric focus wherein standing before God depends on human distinctions, including both ethnicity and personal piety.[47]

The phrase "works of the law" certainly does not exclude Jewish boundary markers, but neither does it reduce to them.[48] The phrase refers to all works demanded by the Mosaic Law.[49] Four observations support this conclusion. First, it is widely agreed that Paul uses the word "works" to denote works in a general sense, whether good or evil. God "will render to each one according to his works," Paul asserts (Rom 2:6). God's election of Jacob over Esau took place before they were born "and had done nothing either good or bad," so that it was "not by works" (Rom 9:11). Paul can speak of the works of darkness (Rom 13:12; Eph 5:11; cf. Col 1:21), the works of the flesh (Gal 5:19), of good works in general (Eph 2:10; 1 Tim 2:10; 5:10, 25; 6:18; 2 Tim 2:21; 3:17; Tit 1:16; 2:7, 14; 3:1, 8, 14) and of false apostles receiving judgment according to their works (2 Cor 11:15; cf. 2 Tim 4:14). All of these examples represent uses of the term "works" with clear moral connotations.

---

45. It must be kept in mind that the term "sinner" in first century Judaism was reserved for the outcasts of society. The term is often paired with "tax collectors" or refers to sexually immoral women (Matt 9:10, 11; 11:19; Mark 2:15, 16; Luke 5:30; 6:32-34; 7:34, 37, 39; 15:1, 2).

46. See Mark A. Seifrid, "Blind Alleys in the Controversy over the Paul of History," *Tyndale Bulletin* 45.1 (1994): 77: "There is little doubt that circumcision, along with obedience to food and Sabbath laws, served Jews as 'boundary markers'. It is highly questionable however, that these 'boundary markers' symbolised *mere* national identity. Ethnic traditions bear values which provide cohesion and continuity in community life. And while early Judaism was a 'national' religion, it was nevertheless a *religion*." Again, on p. 79: "Circumcision symbolised not merely separation from other nations, but an ethically superior monotheism."

47. See Piper's excellent discussion in *The Future of Justification*, 145-61.

48. It must be noted that new perspective proponents do not argue that the phrase "works of the law" refers only to the boundary markers of circumcision, food laws, and Sabbath. As Dunn [*The Theology of Paul the Apostle*, 358] notes, the phrase "does, of course, refer to all or whatever the law requires" (cf. Wright, *Romans*, 460). The significance of this debate, then, is really not over the denotation of the phrase but rather its connotation. New perspective proponents insist that the connotation of the phrase lies exclusively in its boundary-defining role and not in any sense in deeds of merit that boost one's standing before God. So for all practical purposes, they do reduce the significance of the phrase to precepts of the law that define Jews over against Gentiles.

49. The following discussion leans on the insights of Thomas R. Schreiner, *The Law and Its Fulfillment: A Pauline Theology of Law* (Grand Rapids: Baker, 1993), 51-57.

Second, the phrase "works of the law" in Romans 3:28 clearly means the same thing as "works" in the surrounding context. The parallel structure of 3:27-31 and 4:1-25 shows this to be the case, for in chapter 4 Paul unpacks four claims he has made in 3:27-31:

| | | |
|---|---|---|
| faith excludes boasting | 3:27 | 4:1-2 |
| faith is necessary to preserve grace | 3:28 | 4:3-8 |
| faith is necessary if Jews and Gentiles alike are to be saved | 3:29-30 | 4:9-17 |
| Christian faith, then, far from overturning the OT, fulfills the OT anticipation[50] | 3:31 | 4:18-25 |

If it can be established that "works" in Romans 4 refers (as elsewhere in Paul) to works in a general sense, then a compelling case would be made for seeing "works of the law" in 3:28 (and by implication elsewhere) as connoting (not just denoting) good works done in obedience to the Mosaic Law, not merely boundary markers of Jewish identity. This argument stands firm on the use of the term "works" in Romans 4:2, 4, and 6. Paul establishes that Abraham was not justified by works (v. 2) but rather by faith (v. 3). He then elucidates the principle (observed earlier) that righteousness comes as a gift of grace, not as a wage earned (vv. 4-5). As if this were not enough to establish that the term "works" clearly denotes (and connotes!) works performed to achieve a good standing before God, verse 6 solidifies the case: "just as David also speaks of the blessing of the one to whom God counts righteousness apart from works." The quote that follows from Psalm 32 (vv. 7-8) has nothing to do with defining the covenant people of God apart from ethnic considerations but everything to do with forgiveness of sins. Whereas Abraham might suffice as an example of a "Gentile" who was justified apart from "works" as Jewish boundary markers (because he was justified prior to being circumcised, vv. 9-12), David in no way satisfies this criterion, for he bore all the outward marks of Jewish identity, and yet he still had no works to plead his case before God. In what sense, then, could David have been counted righteous apart from works? The only satisfactory answer from the context is that David's sins were forgiven and he was accepted as righteous before God by faith and not on the basis of good works he had performed.[51] The tight connection between the arguments of 3:27-31 and chapter 4 implies, then, that "works of the law" in 3:28 (and by implication in 3:20) must refer to works demanded by the law in general, without the exclusive connotation of Jewish identity markers.

Third, within the context of Galatians there is good reason to see the phrase "works of the law" as encompassing all things demanded by the Mosaic Law, without a primary focus on Jewish identity markers. In 3:10 Paul writes, "For all who rely on

---

50. Carson, "The Vindication of Imputation," 63.

51. See Simon J. Gathercole, *Where Is Boasting? Early Jewish Soteriology and Paul's Response in Romans 1-5* (Grand Rapids: Eerdmans, 2002), 247: "*It is crucial to recognize that the New Perspective interpretation of 4:1-8 falls to the ground on this point: that David although circumcised, sabbatarian, and kosher, is described as without works because of disobedience*" (emphasis original).

works of the law are under a curse; for it is written, 'Cursed be everyone who does not abide by all things written in the Book of the Law, and do them.'" Paul's logic in this verse has been debated, for on the surface it is not obvious why he quotes Deuteronomy 27:26, which pronounces a curse on those who disobey the law, in order to prove the point that all who rely on the law (by obeying it) are under a curse. Dunn argues that Paul pronounces a curse on those who misuse the law as a boundary marker to exclude Gentiles from the covenant people.[52] However, it is highly unlikely that Paul would envision the curses of Deuteronomy 27-29 falling on Israel for an exclusive attitude rather than for disobedience to the precepts of the law itself. Wright argues that Paul's logic builds on the narrative of Israel's history, so that he pronounces a curse on all those who attach themselves to Israel-in-exile by taking on Jewish identity markers ("works of the law").[53] His view founders on a too heavy reliance on the continuing exile theme in Second Temple Judaism.[54] Furthermore, when taken on its own terms, Wright's view renders Paul's argument vulnerable to his opponents. For if Paul and the Judaizers shared a common understanding of Israel's continuing exile, as well as a common understanding that Jesus the Messiah had brought the exile to an end, then what would stop the Judaizers from pressing for Torah observance even more by claiming that the end of the exile marked the occasion to go back to the law and get it right this time around?[55]

In light of the failure of the alternatives, it is best to retain the traditional interpretation of Galatians 3:10, which holds that Paul has left unstated a premise that makes his argument coherent: human inability.[56] The reason why those who rely on works of the law are under a curse is because the curse pronounced in Deuteronomy 27:26 applies to all sinful human beings for their inability to keep the law. Therefore, Paul explicates "works of the law" in terms of "all things written in the Book of the Law," not just the outward signs that mark off Jews from Gentiles.[57] Paul's argument

---

52. James D. G. Dunn, "Works of the Law and the Curse of the Law (Galatians 3.10-14)" in *The New Perspective on Paul: Collected Essays* (Tübingen: Mohr Siebeck, 2005), 111-30; idem, *A Commentary on the Epistle to the Galatians* (London: A & C Black, 1993), 170-74.

53. Wright, *The Climax of the Covenant*, 137-56.

54. For a critique of this view, see Mark A. Seifrid, *Christ, Our Righteousness: Paul's Theology of Justification* (Downers Grove: InterVarsity, 2000), 21-25; idem, "Blind Alleys," 86-92;

55. Seyoon Kim, *Paul and the New Perspective: Second Thoughts on the Origin of Paul's Gospel* (Grand Rapids; Eerdmans, 2002), 136-41.

56. Martin Luther, *Commentary on Galatians*, Modern English Edition (Grand Rapids: Fleming H. Revell, 1988), 159-89; Moisés Silva, *Interpreting Galatians: Explorations in Exegetical Method*, 2nd ed. (Grand Rapids: Baker Academic, 2001), 217-35; Schreiner, *The Law and Its Fulfillment*, 44-63; Steve Jeffery, Mike Ovey, and Andrew Sach, *Pierced for Our Transgressions: Rediscovering the Glory of Penal Substitution* (Nottingham: IVP, 2007), 89-95; F. F. Bruce *The Epistle to the Galatians: A Commentary on the Greek Text*, New International Greek Testament Commentary (Grand Rapids: Eerdmans, 1982), 157-67.

57. Significantly, the MT does not include the word "all" in Deuteronomy 27:26. This indicates that Paul either added the word himself or deliberately chose to quote this portion of the verse from the LXX. Either way, Paul's intention seems to be to emphasize the full range of the Mosaic legislation.

in verses 11-12 substantiates this observation. In verse 11 Paul argues from Habakkuk 2:4 that justification comes by faith, not by the law, and then in verse 12 he shows why the two ways of righteousness are mutually exclusive: "But the law is not of faith, rather 'The one who does them shall live by them'" (cf. Rom 10:5). Here he draws a boundary around the law, indicating, as he does in Romans 4:1-8, that doing and believing are mutually exclusive principles in the realm of justification. "Works of the law" fall under the category of "doing" (Lev 18:5), which stands in contradiction to God's method of justification by grace through faith. Confirmation of this reading comes from Galatians 5:3, where Paul argues that taking on the identity marker of circumcision obligates one to obey the whole law, an obligation that Paul apparently believes should not be taken on because of the impossibility of fulfilling it.

The fourth and final observation in this discussion of "works of the law" has to do with the use of the term "works" in key passages in Ephesians and the Pastoral Epistles.[58] The most significant of these for the present discussion may be found in Titus 3:5-7, where a works/mercy antithesis appears (v. 5) and where believers are said to be justified by God's grace (v. 7). Significantly, Paul writes that God saved us "not because of works done by us in righteousness" (v. 5), clearly indicating that the kinds of works he has in view are good works in a general sense. In a context that mentions justification by grace, the parallel between the works/mercy antithesis and the works of the law/faith antithesis presented elsewhere (Gal 2:16; 3:2, 5; 3:10-14; Rom 3:20-22; 27-28) strongly implies that "works of the law" in Paul belongs in the same sphere of discourse as "works done by us in righteousness," just as "faith" belongs to the realm of "mercy" (see Rom 4:16). The same dynamic appears in Ephesians 2:8-9, where the vocabulary of justification does not appear but the concept seems to be present: "For by grace you have been saved through faith. And this is not your own doing; it is the gift of God, not a result of works so that no one may boast." Here works stand opposed to both grace and faith, and there is no hint that the works mentioned are mere Jewish identity markers.[59] In fact, the reference to "good works" that God has prepared beforehand for believers to do (v. 10) strengthens the observation that the "works" of verse 9 are general in nature. Thus, the antithesis presented in Ephesians 2:8-9 coheres with the traditional Protestant reading of the same kind of antithesis presented in

---

58. Again, while I presuppose, based on my understanding of the nature of inspiration, that Paul wrote these letters, the argument still carries weight even if a later Paulinist (or two or more later Paulinists), seeking to commend Paul's theology to a new generation of believers, actually wrote some or all of them. His/Their interpretation of Paul's theology, standing much closer to Paul in time and culture, surely would not reflect a view that was foreign to Paul.

59. Dunn fully recognizes that "works" in Ephesians 2:9 are good works in general. He argues that a later Paulinist has made explicit the principle of salvation by grace alone that was well-known in Judaism and presupposed by Paul. See Dunn, "Whatever Happened to 'Works of the Law'?" 387-88. But Dunn needs to be pressed on two issues. First, how likely is it that a later Paulinist would use terminology so similar to Paul's, with the same faith/works antithesis, and yet mean something very different from what Paul meant? Second, how might an acceptance of Paul's authorship of Ephesians impact Dunn's reading of Romans and Galatians?

Romans and Galatians. A final verse that deserves mention here is 2 Timothy 1:9, where Paul again draws the antithesis between works and grace in salvation, with no hint that "works" refers to Jewish boundary markers. These observations confirm the argument by highlighting the unlikelihood that Paul would create the same kind of antithesis over and over and yet equivocate on the nature of the contrast.

To sum up these exegetical observations, the notion that Paul's doctrine of justification pertains primarily to marking out the covenant people by the badge of faith rather than by the badge of Jewish identity markers finds little support from his use of the relevant terminology. Righteousness language in Paul refers consistently to ethical and legal realities: those who have fulfilled their ethical obligations are righteous, and those who have not are unrighteous. Justification is the legal recognition that one has fulfilled one's obligations and thus is righteous, although Paul's doctrine of justification by faith departs from this ordinary sense of the term by affirming that God justifies the ungodly, thus granting them a new standing before him because of Christ's redeeming work. Justification by faith, then, cannot be a mere recognition of who is "in"; it must refer to the legal aspect of Christian conversion, a transfer in status from unrighteousness to righteousness. When Paul uses the phrase "works of the law" in opposition to faith, the evidence suggests that he does not envision merely dueling identity markers but that he is driven by the principle outlined in Galatians 3:12 and Romans 4:4-5: the principle of faith, as a passive reception of righteousness, standing over against good works, as an active pursuit of righteousness. Thus, Paul's doctrine of justification has to do primarily with the legal standing of individual sinners before God, not with the definition of God's covenant people. Justification belongs in the realm of soteriology, not ecclesiology.

## Ecclesiological Implications

But does Paul's doctrine of justification have anything to say to ecclesiology? The answer is an emphatic "Yes!" In spite of its deficiencies, the new perspective has done the church a service by drawing attention to the ecclesiological context in which Paul's doctrine of justification was expounded, especially in the letter to the Galatians. Careful attention to Paul's argument demonstrates how the doctrine of justification, while not directly an element of ecclesiology, impacts the nature of the church by summoning believers of various backgrounds to cross human barriers (preeminently the Jew-Gentile barrier) and accept one another as God has accepted them in Christ. A robust doctrine of justification by grace alone through faith alone implies a church that is international in character, drawn from every caste of society, and united together in love because of their mutual recognition that human distinctions mean nothing under the shadow of the cross.

Paul's report of his confrontation with Peter illustrates this point. When Peter, joined by Barnabas and the other Jews at Antioch, withdrew from table fellowship with the Gentiles, Paul confronted him with this question: "If you, though a Jew, have eternal life in the manner of a Gentile and not in the manner of a Jew, how can you force the Gentiles to Judaize?" (Gal 2:14).[60] Peter's act of withdrawal implied that he expected the Gentile believers to put themselves under the Jewish law before he would resume table fellowship with them, thereby indirectly forcing them to become Jews. Significantly, Paul expounded his argument by appealing to the doctrine of justification by faith rather than by works of the law (vv. 15-16). The implication of his argument is that believers should not exclude one another on the basis of human distinctions that do not affect one's legal standing before God. Jews who abandon faith in the law and seek justifying grace in Christ alone admit that they are sinners on the same level with Gentiles (v. 17).[61] The common sinful condition they share before God, along with their common basis of acceptance before him, leads to a practice of mutual acceptance. Justification by faith, once it is grasped as a glorious vertical reality, also reaches out horizontally.

A similar dynamic appears to be at work in Romans 2:29, where Paul suddenly asks the question, "Or is God the God of Jews only?" Wright argues that this question makes no sense if the boast of verse 27 is that of "the successful moralist." It must be, he maintains, "the racial boast of the Jew" over against the Gentile.[62] Along with a truncated view of boasting,[63] this interpretation fails to note the logic of the traditional interpretation. The oneness of God (v. 30) implies that there is only one way of to be right with him, and that is the way of faith as opposed to works of the law, so that it is open to all, both Jews and Gentiles (vv. 27-29).[64] If, therefore, God is one, and there is only one "universally accessible and universally humbling way of justification,"[65] then Jews and Gentiles have no basis on which to exclude each other (see also Eph 2:1-22).

Now that the Jew-Gentile question lies in the distant past, how do churches today apply the doctrine of justification by faith to their ecclesiological practice? They do it by fostering unity in the gospel alone, which stretches across the diverse spectrum of human communities, rather than by gathering into intentionally monolithic congregations. Churches that exist in ethnically diverse areas should strive to reflect the same kind of ethnic diversity as their surroundings. The same goes for diversity in socioeconomic status. Rather than catering to the wealthy, churches should recognize that all sinners stand on level ground before the cross. In light of Paul's teaching, niche churches seem very problematic. While certain churches may have special

60. My translation. Although most English translations do not reflect it, I take the verb "live" in Gal 2:14 to mean in a spiritual sense, as in "have eternal life."

61. Bruce, 140-41.

62. Wright, *What Saint Paul Really Said*, 129; idem, *Romans*, 480-82.

63. See Gathercole, *Where Is Boasting?*, for an extended argument that boasting in this context is directed both toward God and the Gentiles and that it is based both on Israel's election and obedience to the law.

64. Piper, *The Future of Justification*, 146-47.

65. Ibid., 147.

opportunities to minister to particular groups (college students, factory workers, military personnel, ethnic groups, etc.), it seems that the attempt to begin a new church for the specific purpose of reaching only one segment of a diverse society runs counter to the horizontal dimension of justification by faith.[66] Churches that unify because of their common backgrounds or interests run the risk of defining themselves by those human features rather than by the gospel.

There is also a moral dimension to this discussion. Sinners saved by grace must have open arms for other sinners. A church made up of morally respectable justified sinners (e.g., suburbanites whose sins are less public or less shocking than those of others) denies the gospel if it refuses to welcome the "tax collectors and sinners" of its society. May the church be a place for recovering alcoholics, the sexually broken, and juvenile delinquents, for by faith the perfect righteousness of Christ covers their sins every bit as much as it does anyone else's. And may the practice of patience, love, and forgiveness characterize the human-human relationship within the church just as it does the divine-human relationship. Piper's observation about marriage could just as easily apply to relationships between believers in the church:

> What makes marriage almost impossible at times is that both partners feel so self-justified in their expectations that are not being fulfilled. There is a horrible emotional dead-end street in the words, "But it's just plain wrong for you to act that way," followed by, "That's your perfectionistic perspective," or "Do you think you do everything right?," or hopeless, resigned silence. The cycle of self-justified self-pity and anger seems unbreakable.
>
> But what if one or both of the partners becomes overwhelmed with the truth of justification by faith alone, and with the particular truth that in Christ Jesus God credits me, for Christ's sake, as fulfilling all his expectations? What would happen if this doctrine so mastered our souls that we began to bend it from the vertical to the horizontal? What if we applied it to our marriages?[67]

And what if we labored to view our brothers and sisters in the church through the lens of the grace that we ourselves have received? Justification by faith speaks volumes about what the church should be.

## Conclusion

The ecclesiological insights provided by the new perspective on Paul are not wrong in themselves. Jews and Gentiles are indeed united together under one God by faith in one common Savior, where ethnic badges mean nothing. Paul's concern to uphold

---

66. I am by no means opposing the attempts by missionaries to target specific unreached people groups for evangelism, so long as the aim of the ministry is to plant churches that will in time develop a missional outlook that seeks out and welcomes outsiders.

67. John Piper, *Counted Righteous in Christ: Should We Abandon the Imputation of Christ's Righteousness?* (Wheaton: Crossway, 2002), 27.

this glorious truth cannot be denied. However, in their exposition of the doctrine of justification in Paul's writings, new perspective proponents tend to skip an important step on their way to Jew-Gentile unity: the sinner's relationship to God. Yet the evidence from Paul's letters indicates that justification is primarily soteriological, addressing the predicament of guilty sinners before a holy God, delivering them from his wrath, ending the hostility, and creating peace (Rom 5:1, 9-11). Only when this crucial vertical dimension is grasped can one proceed to specify the important implications for ecclesiology. If justification by faith is the answer, then what really is the question? It would seem to be something like this: "How can guilty sinners escape their awful predicament and stand in the right before God?" And sinners who have found that answer cannot help but become channels of grace to one another.

# The Cruciform Shape of Paul's Kingdom Theology

## David Burnette

David Burnette (Ph.D. The Southern Baptist Theological Seminary) works as an editor for Radical, the resource ministry of David Platt

**Abstract:** Unlike Jesus, Paul is not often associated with the theme of the kingdom of God. While some scholars have claimed that the kingdom is insignificant for Paul, most have simply failed to examine it closely. This article highlights the significance of the kingdom by demonstrating that it is a foundational component of Paul's proclamation of the cross. This thesis is based primarily on a close examination of 1 Corinthians 4:20, a verse in which Paul contrasts the talk of certain leaders in Corinth with the power of the kingdom. Based on the way Paul uses the term power (δύναμις, *dynamis*) in 1 Corinthians 1-4, this article contends that the power of the kingdom mentioned in 4:20 is a reference to the power effected through the word of the cross. Other Pauline kingdom references are cited to support this kingdom-cross connection, including Colossians 1:13 and Galatians 5:21. As with the Gospels and Scripture as a whole, Paul's theology of the kingdom is bound up with a message that cuts against the grain of the world's wisdom—the message of Christ crucified.

**Key Words:** kingdom, cross, Paul, power, and 1 Corinthians.

## Introduction

Few themes in Scripture have received as much scholarly attention as the kingdom of God.[1] This preoccupation with the kingdom is understandable, as both John the Baptist and Jesus began their respective public ministries by announcing the kingdom's arrival (Matt 3:2; 4:17) and the kingdom continues to feature prominently throughout the Synoptic Gospels. When we turn to Paul's letters, on the other hand, the kingdom seems less conspicuous. Scholars have given various explanations for this

---

1. Over ten thousand publications related to the kingdom of God have been appeared in the last century alone. Leslaw Daniel Chrupcala, *The Kingdom of God: A Bibliography of 20th Century Research* (Jerusalem: Franciscan Printing Press, 2007), cited in Robert Yarborough, "The Kingdom of God in the New Testament: Matthew and Revelation," in *The Kingdom of God*, ed. Christopher W. Morgan and Robert A. Peterson (Wheaton: Crossway, 2012), 95.

phenomenon, including the idea that Paul intentionally avoided the topic or that he supplanted the kingdom with other emphases.[2] Bultmann claimed that the kingdom "lost its dominant position in Paul,"[3] while Walter goes so far as to say that Paul shows "no trace of the influence of the theologically central affirmations of Jesus' preaching, in particular of his characteristic 'Jesuanic' interpretation of the kingdom of God."[4] It is fair to say that the kingdom has not been a key theme in Pauline studies.

## Connecting the Kingdom and the Cross

Many scholars today reject the idea that Jesus and Paul had completely different messages—a view that used to surface more in the older Jesus versus Paul comparisons. Relatively few scholars, however, have examined Paul's view of the kingdom in a detailed, exegetical manner, which could be taken to imply that the kingdom is not a significant theme in the apostle's writings.[5] In response, I believe there are multiple lines of evidence to suggest that scholars have underestimated this theme in Paul's writings.[6] One way to make this case is by demonstrating the relationship between the kingdom and other central Pauline themes, many of which revolve around God's saving work in Christ.[7] In this article I will be focusing specifically on the relationship between the kingdom and the cross, as this latter theme is universally recognized to be a signature theme in Paul's letters. More specifically, I will examine 1 Corinthians 4:20, along with other supporting examples, in order to demonstrate that the kingdom of God is a foundational aspect of Paul's proclamation of the cross.

Before moving to exegesis, it is worth noting several reasons why 1 Corinthians 4:20 is well suited to my thesis. First, as I intend to demonstrate below, Paul binds the kingdom and the cross inseparably in this verse. Second, while the kingdom is

---

2. For more on the various explanations concerning Paul's lack of emphasis on the kingdom, see my survey in Samuel D. Burnette, "The Kingdom in 1 Corinthians: Reevaluating an Underestimated Pauline Theme" (Ph.D. diss., The Southern Baptist Theological Seminary, 2015), 6-14. It has been claimed that Paul supplanted the kingdom with themes such righteousness, the Spirit, and Christ.

3. Bultmann, *Theology of the New Testament*, 1:189. This shift in emphasis is for Bultmann part of a larger pattern in Paul's theology. The apostle's teaching is not a recapitulation or further development of Jesus' own preaching, but rather a "new structure" suited to a new Hellenized context (189). Lüdemann also questions the significance of the kingdom for Paul, calling it "marginal." Gerd Lüdemann, *Paul, the Founder of Christianity* (Amherst, NY: Prometheus Books, 2002), 194.

4. Nikolaus Walter, "Paul and the Early Christian Jesus-Tradition," in *Paul and Jesus: Collected Essays*, ed. A. J. M. Wedderburn, JSNTSup 37 (Sheffield: Sheffield Academic Press, 1989), 63.

5. For a thorough treatment of the Pauline conception of the kingdom, see the wide-ranging study of Gary Shogren, "The Pauline Proclamation of the Kingdom of God and the Kingdom of Christ Within Its New Testament Setting" (Ph.D. diss., University of Aberdeen, 1986).

6. I have made a case for the significance of the kingdom in 1 Corinthians in Burnette, "The Kingdom in 1 Corinthians: Reevaluating an Underestimated Pauline Theme."

7. Thielman lists several proposed centers for Pauline theology by various scholars, most of which revolve around some aspect of God's salvation in Christ. Frank Thielman, *Theology of the New Testament: A Canonical and Synthetic Approach* (Grand Rapids: Zondervan, 2005), 231.

often related to ethics, to the Spirit, and even to themes like the resurrection[8] in Paul's theology, the cross seems to be on the periphery of such discussions. I do not intend to downplay these other themes nor do I think they can be separated from the cross, but it is worth examining how the kingdom relates (specifically) to a central Pauline theme like the cross. Third, the relationship between the kingdom and the cross in 1 Corinthians 4:20 may not be immediately obvious to all readers given that the term cross (σταυρὸς, *stauros*) does not appear in this verse. I intend to show that the term is implied in the immediate context. Finally, 1 Corinthians 4:20 is a prime example of the role the kingdom plays in Paul's theology. It is my contention, which I cannot defend in the space of this article, that the kingdom serves not as *the* center of Paul's theology, nor even that Paul frequently features it as the subjection of discussion, but rather that it functions like a strong but unobtrusive foundation that supports more prominent structures, structures such as the cross of Christ.[9] Yarbrough makes a similar observation, comparing the kingdom to "an invisible software program running at all times in the background as Paul ministers and from time to time composes his letters."[10] This less conspicuous role for the kingdom may be one reason that scholars have typically underestimated its significance in Paul's writings.

## Examining 1 Corinthians 4:20

In 1 Corinthians 4:20 Paul declares, "For the kingdom of God does not consist in talk but in power." In order to demonstrate the connection between the kingdom and the cross in this verse, a brief look at the wider context of 1 Corinthians 1-4 will be instructive. After his opening greeting and prayer of thanksgiving (1:1-9), Paul admonishes the Corinthians for their divisiveness. Some believers in Corinth were apparently clamoring for spiritual status by identifying with prominent church leaders

---

8. Beale argues that throughout Paul's letters Christ's resurrection establishes the "inaugurated end-time new-creational kingdom." G.K. Beale, *A New Testament Biblical Theology: The Unfolding of the Old Testament in the New* (Grand Rapids: Baker Academic, 2011), 249. See pp. 249-97 for Beale's exegesis of the relevant texts related to the resurrection as the inaugural eschatological event in Paul's letters.

9. I have identified several ways in which the kingdom is foundational to God's saving work in Christ in 1 Corinthians in Burnette, "The Kingdom in 1 Corinthians: Reevaluating an Underestimated Pauline Theme."

10. Robert Yarbrough, "The Kingdom of God in the New Testament: Mark through the Epistles," in *The Kingdom of God*, ed. Christopher W. Morgan and Robert A. Peterson (Wheaton, IL: Crossway, 2012), 148.

like Paul and Apollos (1:10-17).[11] Paul responds to this jockeying by highlighting the word of the cross in 1:18ff, for those who have believed in a crucified Messiah should eschew the world's views of power and wisdom. True wisdom is revealed by the Spirit and it hails from the age to come (2:6-13), thus making it folly to the "natural person" (2:14). The issue of divisiveness over leaders continues to surface in 3:1-5, leading Paul to remind the Corinthians that he and Apollos were merely servants who watered. God is responsible for the growth, i.e., effectiveness in ministry (3:5-7). In chapter 4 the imagery shifts slightly, but the general topic is the same. Paul and Apollos are now described as stewards of God's mysteries, and while stewards must be found faithful, it is God's judgment (and not that of the Corinthians) that counts in such matters (4:1-5). In 4:6-7 Paul confronts the arrogance of the Corinthians by reminding them that any distinctions or gifts they possess are from God. Moreover, the very apostles the Corinthians were elevating had become "a spectacle to the world, to angels, and to men" (v. 9). Paul thus sets the pride and posturing of the Corinthians in sharp contrast to the suffering and ridicule experienced by the apostles (4:8-13). The fact that the apostles looked unimpressive to the world helps set the stage for Paul's comments about the kingdom in 4:20.

Paul admonishes the Corinthians in 4:14-21 concerning their "countless guides in Christ" (v. 15).[12] Some in Corinth became arrogant in Paul's absence, supposing the apostle would not come to correct them (v.18). However, Paul did respond to these arrogant persons in verses 19-20, citing the power of the kingdom to make his case. With this broader context in mind, Paul's reference to the "power" (δύναμις,

---

11. Mitchell takes 1:10 to be the thesis statement for the overall argument of 1 Corinthians, which is an argument for ecclesial unity. M. M. Mitchell, *Paul and the Rhetoric of Reconciliation: An Exegetical Investigation of the Language and Composition of 1 Corinthians*, (Louisville: Westminster/John Knox Press, 1993), 1. Likewise Collins claims that Paul's warning against divisions in 1:10 "makes a statement that defines the rest of the letter." Raymond F. Collins, *First Corinthians*, Sacra Pagina (Collegeville, MN: Liturgical Press, 1999), 69. Ciampa and Rosner argue that while disunity is a major theme in the letter, there are other "equally important concerns." Roy E. Ciampa and Brian Rosner, *The First Letter to the Corinthians*, PNTC (Grand Rapids: Eerdmans, 2010), 73. Ciampa and Rosner note, "… Paul must seek not only to unify the Corinthian Christians but, just as importantly, to rid them of pagan influences other than disunity, in particular sexual immorality (cf. 6:18), idolatry (cf. 10:14), and greed. Paul's task is to seek the Corinthians' transformation by the renewing of their mind, so that they might live lives that are holy (1 Cor. 1:2) and pleasing to God (Rom 12:2; Titus 2:11-13)" (74).

12. On the importance of 1 Cor 4:6-21 for the rest of the epistle, see E. Coye Still, "Divisions Over Leaders and Food Offered to Idols," *Tyndale Bulletin* 55 (2004): 17-41. Although Still focuses primarily on the thematic parallels between 4:6-21 and 8:1-11, he offers support for Dahl's theory that the "theological basis for Paul's answers to the problems of 1 Cor 5-15 is set forth in chapters 1-4, and calls attention especially to 4:6-21 as foundational to Paul's understanding of Christian existence in community" (41). Dahl's theory can be found in Nils A. Dahl, "Paul and the Church at Corinth According to 1 Corinthians 1:10-4:21," in *Christian History and Interpretation*, ed. W. R. Farmer, C. F. D. Moule, and R.R. Niebuhr (Cambridge, MA: University Press, 1967), 313-35. Ciampa and Rosner are in the minority of commentators in terms of taking 4:18-21 with the next section of this epistle, which stretches from 4:18 to 6:20. (Ciampa and Rosner, *The First Letter to the Corinthians*, 189–91). While this structuring of the passage is certainly plausible, this matter does not significantly affect one's understanding of the kingdom in 4:20.

*dynamis*) of the kingdom and its relationship to the cross in 4:19-20 can now be examined more closely.

## The Power of the Kingdom

Paul's claim about the power of the kingdom in 4:20 must be understood in light of his challenge to the arrogant guides in 4:19.[13] Paul claims in 4:19 that the litmus test for spiritual guides in Corinth would not be their "talk" (λόγον, *logon*) but rather their "power" (δύναμιν, *dynamin*). The reason power serves as the standard is that, according to 4:20, the kingdom consists "in power" (ἐν δυνάμει, *en dynamei*).[14] Paul's point is that an approved ministry must manifest the power of God's kingdom. The terms "talk" (λόγος, *logos*) and "power" (δύναμις, *dynamis*) are contrasted in 4:19 and in 4:20,[15] and it is this contrast that Paul uses to characterize the kingdom of God.[16]

Paul's claim that the kingdom does not consist in "talk" (λόγῳ, *logō*) in 4:19-20 initially seems to run against my argument that the power of the kingdom is manifest through the "word (λόγος, *logos*) of the cross" (1:18). After all, the word of the cross is by definition a *verbal* proclamation and would therefore seem to fall under the category of talk. However, Schrage rightly notes that the immediate and wider context of 1 Corinthians 1-4 makes it clear that Paul is not disparaging verbal proclamation *per se*.[17] In fact, a certain kind of verbal proclamation is indispensable to the apostle's purposes and calling. For example, Paul is a steward of the mysteries of God (4:1), and he has fathered the Corinthian believers "through the gospel" (4:15). The wider context makes this point as well, for Paul speaks of the character and content of his verbal proclamation in 2:1-4. Christ sent him to "preach the gospel" (1:17), and it is the "word (λόγος, *logos*) of the cross" which God uses to save the foolish and the weak among both Jews and Greeks (1:18-31). Furthermore, in 2:13 Paul claims to impart wisdom via "words" (λόγοις, *logois*) that must be taught and interpreted by the Spirit. Clearly, then, the apostle is not denigrating verbal proclamation in an absolute sense.

---

13. Conzelmann rightly notes that 4:20 is the ground for 4:19. Hans Conzelmann, *1 Corinthians: A Commentary on the First Epistle to the Corinthians*, Hermeneia (Philadelphia: Fortress Press, 1975), 93.

14. Paul's statement in 4:20 is elliptical, with the ESV and NASB supplying the verb "consists" to characterize the relationship of the kingdom to "talk" and "power."

15. So Schrage, who seeks to derive the meaning of δύναμις (*dynamis*, power) from this contrast. Wolfgang Schrage, *Der erste Brief an die Korinther*, EKKNT 7 (Zürich: Benziger; Neukirchen-Vluyn: Neukirchener, 1991), 1:362–63.

16. Haufe rightly notes that Paul is not giving a full definition of the kingdom in 4:20 but rather an important feature of it. Haufe, "Reich Gottes bei Paulus," 469. Likewise Donfried has noted that the immediate context in 1 Corinthians has influenced what Paul chose to say about the kingdom: "It [1 Cor 4:20] is concentrating on one dimension of that new reality in light of certain misunderstandings present in the Corinthian congregation. Karl Donfried, "The Kingdom of God in Paul," in *The Kingdom of God in 20th-Century Interpretation*, ed. Wendell L. Willis (Peabody, MA: Hendrickson, 1987), 179.

17. Schrage, *Der erste Brief an die Korinther*, 1:362–63.

For, as Pogoloff points out, Paul himself uses rhetoric in the very passages in which he rejects its abuse.[18] It still remains, then, to find out specifically what Paul means when he speaks of the "talk" (λόγος, *logos*) of certain persons in Corinth.

**Examining the term** λόγος **(*logos*).** In order to understand how Paul is using the term λόγος (*logos*) in 4:19-20, a distinction must be made between the two uses of the term in 1 Corinthians 1-4. In 1:18, for example, the λόγος (*logos,* word) of the cross is said to be the "power of God" to those who are being saved. This use of λόγος (*logos*) is close to the English concepts of message and proclamation, terms that carry no necessary negative connotations for Paul. On the other hand, Paul uses the term with a negative connotation in 4:19-20, which may help explain why this is the only place in 1 Corinthians 1-4 that the ESV translates the term as "talk" rather than "word." Another example of a negative use of λόγος (*logos,* word) occurs in 1:17, where Paul says he was not sent to preach the gospel with "words of eloquent wisdom" (ἐν σοφίᾳ λόγου, *en sophia logu*). Ciampa and Rosner correctly note that Paul is contrasting "mere words or rhetorical artistry, and the power of God to change lives and destinies."[19] This conclusion is supported by Pogoloff's study on the role of rhetoric in the Corinthian context.[20] There is, therefore, good reason to believe that in 4:19-20 Paul uses the term λόγον (*logon*) to refer to talk or rhetoric that is characterized by worldly wisdom and eloquence. Such talk, Paul says, has nothing to do with the power of the kingdom.

**Examining the term** δύναμις **(*dynamis*).** If Paul's use of the term λόγος (*logos*) in 4:19-20 refers to the kind of eloquent wisdom prized by the world, then there are significant implications for the meaning of the term δύναμις (*dynamis*) and the kind of power that characterizes the kingdom. Marshall claims that it was common for the term δύναμις (*dynamis*) to be associated with rhetoric in a first-century Greco-Roman context to denote "strength, power, influence."[21] Such an association would add

---

18. Stephen M. Pogoloff, *Logos and Sophia: The Rhetorical Situation of 1 Corinthians*, SBLDS 134 (Atlanta: Scholars Press, 1992), 121.

19. Ciampa and Rosner, *The First Letter to the Corinthians*, 195. A similar contrast appears in 2:4-5, where "plausible words of wisdom" are contrasted with the "demonstration of the Spirit and of power" (v.4).

20. See Stephen M. Pogoloff, *Logos and Sophia: The Rhetorical Situation of 1 Corinthians*. Pogoloff examines how rhetoric and eloquence are linked with status in Paul's Greco-Roman context, claiming that Paul has "radically reversed" these cultural narratives. "What persuades is speech about what is ordinarily unfit for contemplation: not a life which is cultured, wise, and powerful, but one marked by the worst shame and the lowest possible status. Paul's rhetoric of the cross thus opposes the cultural values surrounding eloquence" (Pogoloff, *Logos and Sophia*, 120). Litfin examines Paul's proclamation in light of Greco-Roman rhetoric and comes to a similar conclusion. Litfin, *St. Paul's Theology of Proclamation*, 244–62.

21. Peter Marshall, *Enmity in Corinth: Social Conventions in Paul's Relations with the Corinthians*, WUNT 23 (Tübingen: Mohr Siebeck, 1987), 387.

rhetorical force to the contrast Paul draws between the δύναμις (*dynamis*) of God's kingdom and that of traditional Greek rhetoric, the latter being implied in the phrases "lofty speech or wisdom" (2:1) and "plausible words of wisdom" (2:4).[22] Nevertheless, commentators have not always agreed on what Paul means by the term δύναμις (*dynamis*) in this context.[23]

The idea that God's power in 4:20 is a reference to Spirit-produced signs goes back at least as far as Chrysostom.[24] Similarly, Donfried understands the term to refer to "the powerful deeds which accompanied his [Paul's] apostolic preaching."[25] Several Pauline passages are cited to support this understanding, including 1 Corinthians 2:4.[26] Hays speculates that God may need to "unleash some manifestation of the power of the Spirit," something on the order of Elijah's triumph over the prophets of Baal, in order to silence the arrogant in Corinth.[27] The power of the kingdom in 4:20 would thus be akin to God's powerful deeds in the history of Israel. Such interpretations of δύναμις (*dynamis*) in 4:20 are certainly plausible, particularly given the way Paul uses the term in later in 1 Corinthians (6:14; 15:43).[28] However, Paul's emphasis in 1 Corinthians 1-4 on the counter-intuitive manner in which God works through weakness and through a foolish message makes it more likely that the power Paul refers to in 4:20 is related to the proclamation of the cross. I will attempt to demonstrate this point below by examining Paul's previous uses of the term δύναμις (*dynamis*) in 1 Corinthians 1-4.

Prior to 4:19-20, the term δύναμις (*dynamis*) is used five times in 1 Corinthians 1-4: 1:17, 1:18, 1:24, 2:4, and 2:5. In each instance the term is related to the cross. In 1:17 the connection between the cross and power is explicit: relying on "words of eloquent wisdom" means that the cross will be "emptied of its power δύναμις (*dynamis*)." Then in 1:18 Paul says that while the word of the cross is "folly" in the world's estimation, it

---

22. Ibid., 388.

23. For a list of several interpretations offered by scholars concerning Paul's use of the term "power" in 4:20, see William David Spencer, "The Power in Paul's Teaching (1 Cor 4:9-10)," *Journal of the Evangelical Theological Society* 32 (1989): 51-61. Spencer argues that Paul's power is his "display of his life of suffering as an imitation of Christ" (54), which is closer to the position in this work insofar as it distances God's power from worldly conceptions of the concept.

24. Chrysostom, *1 Corinthians Homily 14.2*, trans. A. Roberts and W.H. Rambaut, *ANF*, American ed., vol. 1 (Buffalo, NY: Christian Literature, 1885; repr., Grand Rapids: Eerdmans, 1975), 1: 448.

25. Donfried, "The Kingdom of God in Paul," 180; so Youngmo Cho, *Spirit and Kingdom in the Writings of Luke and Paul: An Attempt to Reconcile These Concepts*, Paternoster Biblical Monographs (Waynesboro, GA; Paternoster, 2005), 58.

26. Donfried, "The Kingdom of God in Paul," 180. See also Rom 15:19; 2 Cor 12:12; 1 Thess 1:5.

27. Richard B. Hays, *First Corinthians*, Interpretation (Louisville: John Knox Press, 1997), 75.

28. Anthony C. Thiselton, *The First Epistle to the Corinthians: A Commentary on the Greek Text*, NIGTC (Grand Rapids: Eerdmans; Carlisle, UK: Paternoster, 2000), 376.

is "the power δύναμις (*dynamis*) of God" to those who are being saved.²⁹ Paul's third use of the term δύναμις (*dynamis*) occurs in 1:24, where Christ himself is referred to as the θεοῦ δύναμιν (*theu dynamin*, power of God). Paul's use of δύναμις (*dynamis*) in 1:24 should be understood in light of the reference to "Christ crucified" in 1:23, which again connects power to the message of the cross.³⁰ The final two occurrences of δύναμις (*dynamis*) in 1 Corinthians 1-4 are in 2:4 and 2:5 respectively. In 2:4 Paul claims that his speech was "in demonstration of the Spirit and of power (δυνάμεως, *dynameōs*)"³¹ and then in 2:5 he says he wants the Corinthians' faith to rest "in the power (δύναμις, *dynamis*) of God." Given that Paul's demonstration of the Spirit and power took place through his proclamation of "Jesus Christ and him crucified" (2:1-2), it is natural to understand the power of the Spirit as being integrally connected to the message of the cross.³² In conclusion, each of Paul's five uses of the term δύναμις (*dynamis*) prior to 4:19-20 is related to the message of the cross.

## Conclusions on the Power of The Kingdom

The exegesis above demonstrates that Paul's use of the term δύναμις (*dynamis*) in 1 Corinthians 1-4 is integrally related to the word of the cross. Though δύναμις

---

29. Garland understands power in 1:18 to refer to "the effectiveness of the cross to make God known to humankind, to accomplish salvation, to defeat evil, and to transform lives and values." David E. Garland, *1 Corinthians*, BECNT (Grand Rapids: Baker Academic, 2003), 62.

30. Similarly, in Romans 1:16 Paul refers to the gospel as the "power" (δύναμις, *dynamis*) of God for salvation to everyone who believes." Like the word of the cross in 1 Corinthians 1-4, the gospel in Romans 1:16 is God's powerful means of bringing about his saving purposes. Moo also draws this parallel between Romans 1:16 and 1 Corinthians 1:18, with both verses connecting the gospel to God's saving power. Douglas J. Moo, *The Epistle to the Romans*, NICNT (Grand Rapids: Eerdmans, 1996), 66. Moo cites 1 Cor 4:19-20 as evidence of the relationship between δύναμις (*dynamis*, power) and the word of the gospel (66 n14), presumably drawing a very close connection between the kingdom and the gospel. Schreiner draws essentially the same connection between Rom 1:16 and 1 Cor 1:18, noting, "The succeeding context of 1 Cor 1 clarifies that the power of the gospel lies in its effective work in calling believers to salvation (1 Cor 1:23-24, 26-29)," (Thomas R. Schreiner, *Romans*, BECNT [Grand Rapids: Baker Books, 1998], 60).

31. Commentators differ over how to understand the phrase "of the Spirit and power" (πνεύματος καὶ δυνάμεως, *pneumatos kai dynameōs*)—whether subjectively (Paul's message was itself a demonstration of the Spirit), objectively (the Spirit's presence was demonstrated through Paul's message), or both—and while a decision is difficult, the meaning of the verse is not affected significantly. Taking the genitives to be objective (ESV and NASB) may be preferable, resulting in a translation such as "in demonstration of the Spirit and of power." Regardless of how one understands these genitives, it is the close relationship between the Spirit and power that is significant. The Spirit is closely associated with power elsewhere in Paul's epistles. For example, see Rom 1:4; 15:13, 19; 1 Thess 1:5. Fee takes the terms "Spirit" and "power" to be close to a hendiadys given their close association in Paul's writings. Gordon D. Fee, *The First Epistle to the Corinthians*, The New International Commentary on the New Testament (Grand Rapids: Eerdmans, 1987), 95. Garland rightly grasps the main point: "What is clear is that Paul attributes the Corinthians' conversion to the powerful intervention of the Spirit." Garland, *1 Corinthians*, 87.

32. Paul's grouping of the same concepts—the Spirit and power—in connection with the gospel in 1 Thessalonians 1:4-5 adds support to this conclusion.

(*dynamis*) could refer to a visible demonstration of power in the form of Spirit-produced signs and wonders, Conzelmann's interpretation fits better with the immediate context: "[Paul] has not forgotten that δύναμις appears in weakness. The power in virtue of which he will put them to the test is no other than the power indicated in 2:1ff."[33] According to 2:4-5, the Spirit is involved in this manifestation of kingdom power through the proclamation of the cross. Thus, to say that the kingdom of God consists in power (rather than talk) is to say that the kingdom is manifest where God's purposes are effected through the proclamation of the cross.[34] Paul is speaking of "effectiveness in life as against mere rhetoric."[35]

## Other Cross-Related Kingdom Texts

One objection to the connection I have drawn between the kingdom and the cross is that 1 Corinthians 4:20 is merely an anomaly in Paul's letters. However, other Pauline kingdom references could be used to make a similar point. In Colossians 1:13, for example, Paul says that the Colossian believers have been transferred to "the kingdom of his [God's] beloved Son," a transfer that involves "redemption, the forgiveness of sins" (Col 1:14).[36] These latter concepts, redemption and forgiveness, clearly imply that Paul has in mind Christ's work on the cross, a connection that is made explicit in the near context by the reference to the "blood of his [Christ's] cross" (v.20). To be transferred into the kingdom, then, is to experience the redemption that comes through Christ's work on the cross. This kingdom-cross connection in Colossians 1:13 is consistent with the idea in 1 Corinthians 4:20 that the power of the kingdom is manifest through the preaching of the cross.

A less obvious connection between the kingdom and the cross occurs in some of Paul's kingdom-inheritance sayings. In Galatians 5:19-21, for example, Paul

---

33. Conzelmann, *1 Corinthians*, 93.

34. Schrage defines power similarly in this context by using the term *Durchschlagskraft*, a reference to the effectiveness of something. Schrage, *Der erste Brief an die Korinther*, 1:362–63. Schreiner strikes a similar note regarding the parallel passage in Rom 1:16-17 noted above. The gospel is the "power (δύναμις, *dynamis*) of God for salvation" (v. 16). The word "for" (εἰς, *eis*) here indicates a result, so that the gospel is God's power resulting in salvation. Schreiner observes, "The δύναμις θεοῦ (*dynamis theu*) in the gospel signifies the effective and transforming power that accompanies the preaching of the gospel." As it relates to 1 Cor 1:18, Schreiner notes that the context of 1 Cor 1:23-24; 26-29 "clarifies that the power of the gospel lies in its effective work in calling believers to salvation" (Schreiner, *Romans*, 60).

35. Thiselton, *The First Epistle to the Corinthians*, 376.

36. Yarbrough notes that this kingdom reference in Col 1:13 serves as a "hinge" connecting the opening sections of the letter (1:3-12 and 15-24), for it "points to the centrality of Paul's kingdom conviction, not only in his understanding but in the outlook of the recently planted Gentile churches. . . . Given the literary placement of Colossians 1:13, it could be argued that the rest of Colossians is a commentary on the meaning of 'kingdom' for the Colossian readers." Yarbrough, "The Kingdom of God in the New Testament: Mark through the Epistles," 147. On the significance of the kingdom in the context of Col 1, see pp.146-47.

lists the "works of the flesh" (v.19) and he says that those who practice such works "will not inherit the kingdom of God" (v.21). The works of the flesh are then contrasted with the fruit of the Spirit (vv.22-23), leading commentators to note the ethics that characterize the kingdom as well as the Spirit's integral role in empowering such righteous conduct.[37] The role of the cross, on the other hand, is less often noticed. But Vickers is right that we should not read Galatians 5:19-21 apart from the previous five chapters, chapters that emphasize faith in Christ's cross-work over against the works of the law. Vickers notes, "Paul's soteriology provides the backdrop for what he has to say about the lives of those who inherit the kingdom in chapter 5."[38] Even in the immediate context the cross is present: those whom the Spirit works through are said to have "crucified the flesh with its passions and desires" (v.24). The term "crucified" has in view Christ's death and, more specifically, the believer's participation in Christ's death whereby the sinful desires of the flesh have been overcome (see also Gal 2:20).[39] The cross is therefore the means by which believers are enabled to inherit the kingdom, a kingdom whose citizens are characterized by Spirit-produced virtues. In addition to the two examples mentioned above, connections between the kingdom and the cross can also be observed in other Pauline kingdom texts.[40] It is also worth noting that Paul's kingdom theology should not be restricted to his use of the noun "kingdom" (βασιλεία, *basileia*). More space could be devoted to the ways in which the cross is related to other kingdom-related concepts, such as the reign of Christ and the reign of believers.[41]

---

37. Vickers notes that the fruit of the Spirit may appropriately be called the "fruit of the kingdom." Brian J. Vickers, "The Kingdom of God in Paul's Gospel," *SBJT* (Spring 2008): 58.

38. Ibid., 58.

39. Commenting on the relationship between the cross and the kingdom in Galatians (and in particular Gal 2:20), Young notes that "the cross is again related to the winding up of the old order, the bearing of the curse and its annulling, so that the promise of the new can be realized. . . . Thus it relates to the fruits of the Spirit and the inheritance of the kingdom." Frances Young, "Paul and the Kingdom of God," in *The Kingdom of God and Human Society*, ed. Robin Barbour (Edinburgh: T&T Clark, 1993), 250.

40. Vickers notes the relationship between the kingdom and the cross in Ephesians 5:1ff, a text that is parallel with Galatians 5:21ff. Prior to listing sins that will disqualify one from the kingdom, Paul mentions that Christ "loved us and gave himself up for us, a fragrant offering and sacrifice to God" (Eph 5:1-2). Here Paul's discussion of the kingdom is "rooted in the cross and resurrection." Vickers, "The Kingdom of God in Paul's Gospel," 59. Commenting on the relationship between the cross and the kingdom in Paul's letters to the Thessalonians, Young makes some broader theological observations: Like Christ, the Christian is marked by "suffering, affliction, and persecution." The cross marks the "destruction of the old order" and it "belongs to the process whereby the kingdom comes into being." Young, "Paul and the Kingdom of God," 250.

41. To take two examples from 1 Corinthians, Paul refers (sarcastically) to the reign of believers in 4:8 and to the reign of Christ in 1 Corinthians 15:25.

## Conclusions and Implications

I have attempted to demonstrate the close relationship between the kingdom and the cross in 1 Corinthians 4:20 in order to draw attention to the significance of the kingdom in Paul's theology. The word of the cross is the means by which the power of the kingdom is effected in this present age. This connection between the kingdom and the cross has also been highlighted in other Pauline texts. To enter the kingdom is to experience the redemption and forgiveness that come through the cross (Col 1:13-14). The cross even makes possible the righteous living required to inherit the kingdom, for the believer's fleshly desires have been crucified with Christ (Gal 5:21-24; Eph 5:2). Paul's view of the kingdom, then, is integrally connected to the cross.

In terms of the broader theological implications for my conclusions, space will only allow me to hint at a couple of points. First, while the kingdom is sometimes considered to be a point of discontinuity between Jesus and Paul, my conclusions suggest otherwise. Paul is remarkably consistent with the Gospels in terms of the relationship between the kingdom and the cross. Treat points out that in Mark's Gospel, for instance, the kingdom comes by "way of the cross."[42] God's power is revealed through the death of the Son of God in much the same way that the power of the kingdom in 1 Corinthians 1-4 is manifested through the message of a crucified Messiah.[43] Similar connections are made in the other Gospels.[44] Second, Paul's cross-shaped view of the kingdom is also consistent with the broader narrative of Scripture. Treat traces the relationship between the kingdom and the cross throughout redemptive history and makes the following observation:

> Although the idea of a 'Messiah crucified seems an oxymoron, in the wisdom of God the promised anointed one of Israel has established God's kingdom by means of the cross. Paul uses power and wisdom, which are traditionally royal characteristics (Ps 145:11; Dan 2:37), to define the message of the cross. In fact, Paul uses "power" to describe both the cross (1 Cor 1:18) and the kingdom (4:20). In a similar way, in the book of Revelation the slain Lamb is praised for his power and his wisdom (Rev 5:12). The kingdom of God comes in power, but the power of the gospel is Christ crucified.[45]

God has a pattern of carrying out his purposes in ways that turn the world's wisdom on its head. It should not be a great surprise, then, that for Paul the kingdom has

---

42. Jeremy R. Treat, *The Crucified King: Atonement and Kingdom in Biblical and Systematic Theology* (Grand Rapids: Zondervan, 2014), 110. For Treat's argument that the kingdom is established by the cross in Mark's Gospel, see pp. 87-110.

43. Ibid., 111. For Treat's argument that the kingdom is established by the cross in Mark's Gospel, see pp. 87-110.

44. Ibid., 111.

45. Ibid., 144.

a "cruciform shape."[46] Whenever the apostle speaks of the cross and its effects and implications, as he so often does, it should be remembered that the power of the kingdom is close at hand.

---

46. The phrase "cruciform shape" is borrowed from Vickers, "The Kingdom of God in Paul's Gospel," 63. Vickers goes further, arguing not only that there is a cruciform shape to Paul's *teaching*, but also to Paul's *life* (cf. 1 Thess 2; 2 Thess 1; 2 Tim 4).

# The Righteousness of God as "The Gate to Paradise": A Review Article of *The Righteousness of God* by Charles Lee Irons

Irons, Charles Lee. *The Righteousness of God: A Lexical Examination of the Covenant-Faithfulness Interpretation*. Wissenschaftliche Untersuchungen zum Neuen Testament 2/386. Tübingen: Mohr Siebeck, 2015. 444 pp.

## Joshua M. Greever

Joshua M. Greever has a PhD in New Testament and teaches New Testament at Grand Canyon University and Grand Canyon Theological Seminary

### Introduction

In approximately the year 1518 Martin Luther discovered the gospel of the righteousness of God. In a preface to his Latin writings in 1545 he recounted his experience, which had to do with his understanding of Romans 1:17:

> Though I lived as a monk without reproach, I felt that I was a sinner before God with an extremely disturbed conscience. I could not believe that he was placated by my satisfaction. I did not love, yes, I hated the righteous God who punishes sinners, and secretly, if not blasphemously, certainly murmuring greatly, I was angry with God....
>
> At last, by the mercy of God, meditating day and night, I gave heed to the context of the words, namely, "In it the righteousness of God is revealed, as it is written, 'He who through faith is righteous will live.'" There I began to understand that the righteousness of God is that by which the righteous live by a gift of God, namely by faith. And this is the meaning: the righteousness of God is revealed by the gospel, namely, the passive righteousness with which merciful God justifies us by faith, as it is written, "He who through faith is righteous shall live." Here I felt that I was altogether born again and had entered paradise itself through open gates....

And I extolled my sweetest word with a love as great as the hatred with which I had before hated the word "righteousness of God." Thus that place in Paul was for me truly the gate to paradise.[1]

Luther's experience is telling: knowing the precise sense of the "righteousness of God" has great import, for it is the difference between "an extremely disturbed conscience" and entrance into "paradise." Over the centuries, Luther has not been alone in wrestling with Paul's meaning, for it has been the focus of much scholarly attention. Not surprisingly, the issues surrounding the "righteousness of God" are thorny and complex. Questions such as the following dominate the discussion:
Is righteousness a relational or covenantal concept, or is it defined as conformity to an external norm?

- Is the righteousness of God to be equated with the righteousness of faith, or does the former produce the latter?
- Is the righteousness of God always and only a positive concept that signifies God's act to save and vindicate his people? More specifically, does God's righteousness connote his covenant faithfulness?
- Does the righteousness of God include God's act to judge those who oppress his people? Does God's righteousness include notions of distributive justice?
- Is the righteousness of God a "gift" to people, such that people can have a divinely-approved righteousness from and before God?

In his published dissertation, *The Righteousness of God: A Lexical Examination of the Covenant-Faithfulness Interpretation*, Charles Lee Irons has provided a much-needed contribution to these questions. Before I review Irons' thesis and arguments as well as offer some constructive critique, I want to make clear at the outset that I am in fundamental agreement with his thesis regarding the righteousness of God. Even though clarity of argument can be better achieved at various points, I believe he has demonstrated convincingly and definitively that God's righteousness is not to be defined as or equated with God's covenant faithfulness, and that Paul's teaching on the righteousness of God primarily concerns the divinely-approved righteousness before God that believers receive by faith in Jesus Christ.

## The Thesis and Argument of *The Righteousness of God*

The thesis of *The Righteousness of God* is inextricably lexical: the Hebrew and Greek terms for righteousness in Scripture (צֶדֶק/צְדָקָה; δικαιοσύνη) do not *mean* faithfulness to covenant promises. That is, righteousness is not a relational concept but concerns

---

[1]. Martin Luther, *Luther's Works: American Edition*, ed. Jaroslav Pelikan and Helmut T. Lehmann (Saint Louis: Concordia, 1972), 34.336-37 (as quoted in Charles Lee Irons, *The Righteousness of God: A Lexical Examination of the Covenant-Faithfulness Interpretation*, Wissenschaftliche Untersuchungen zum Neuen Testament 2/386 [Tübingen: Mohr Siebeck, 2015], 22-23).

conformity to an external norm.[2] Hence, divine righteousness—the "righteousness of God"—does not *mean* that God acts to save in fulfillment of his covenant promises. Furthermore, Paul's teaching on justification—the divine declaration that a person is "righteous"—has little to do with "covenant membership" but rather describes "the state of being legally recognized as δίκαιος ["righteous"] before God."[3] Irons' thesis, therefore, is a shot across the bow towards the so-called "New Perspective on Paul," a rather recent interpretive tradition that has emphasized the covenantal/sociological/ecclesiological nature of God's righteousness and an individual's justification.

The argument of the book is logical and easy to follow. Chapter 1 surveys the history of interpretation regarding the righteousness of God. Irons concludes that until the middle of the 19th century, church theologians interpreted the righteousness of God as a gift. Precisely *how* the righteousness is given was debated—whether it was infused or imputed—but that it was *given* was a source of agreement. In the middle of the 19th century there arose a new strain of interpretation, associated with names like Albrecht Ritschl and Hermann Cremer, which defined righteousness either in relation to God's love or as a relational and covenantal term. This new school of thought undergirded such 20th century interpreters as Ernst Käsemann, who contended for the power-character instead of the gift-character of God's righteousness, as well as the scholars associated with the New Perspective on Paul, such as James D. G. Dunn and N. T. Wright, who define God's righteousness as his faithfulness to save his people in fulfillment of his covenant promises.

After Chapter 2 lays out the method and ground rules for the succeeding chapters, Chapters 3-5 analyze righteousness language in extra-biblical Greek, the Old Testament, and Jewish literature of the Second Temple period. In Chapter 3 on righteousness terminology in extra-biblical Greek, Irons shows that righteousness is often used with an ethical sense as a cardinal virtue, and sometimes it can be used in the sense of distributive justice.

In Chapter 4 Irons analyzes righteousness language in the Hebrew Bible as well as the Septuagint. He finds that there are two primary semantic distinctions for righteousness terminology—a legal and an ethical sense—although he adds a third category of "correctness" as well. At times the legal and ethical senses can blend together, though, especially when righteousness describes an individual's righteous status before God.[4] This righteousness-before-God can be attained by actual ethical righteousness or by God's gracious accrediting of righteousness.[5] Chapter 4 is one of the most

---

2. "There is no evidence, in either the Greek or the Hebrew usage, for the notion that 'righteousness' is a relational concept in which the relationship itself is the norm so that 'righteousness' is conformity to the demands that a relationship brings with itself" (Irons, *The Righteousness of God*, 8).

3. Ibid., 7.

4. The ethical category "can refer simply to righteous conduct, often with verbs of doing, or to the status of righteousness that one has in God's eyes on the basis of such righteous conduct" (ibid., 118).

5. Ibid., 118, 124.

significant in the book, for the Old Testament's use of righteousness serves as the most likely background for Paul's understanding of the righteousness of God.

In Chapter 5 Irons examines righteousness terminology in the Jewish literature of the Second Temple period, such as the Dead Sea Scrolls, Jewish apocryphal and pseudepigraphical writings originally composed in Hebrew (e.g., Psalms of Solomon, Jubilees, 1 Enoch), Jewish apocryphal and pseudepigraphical writings originally composed in Greek (e.g., Wisdom of Solomon, Philo, Josephus), and the New Testament (outside of Paul's letters). Although there are various shades of meaning that each stream of literature emphasizes concerning righteousness, Irons concludes that there is much continuity between the use of righteousness language in the Old Testament and that in the Second Temple literature. However, Irons notes that there seems to be more emphasis in this literature on obtaining and/or maintaining a righteousness before God by strict adherence to the law of Moses—an emphasis Paul will attack in his emphasis on righteousness by faith.

Finally, Chapter 6 is the climactic chapter in which Irons analyzes Paul's ten occurrences of the phrase "righteousness of God" (δικαιοσύνη θεοῦ) against the backdrop of the semantic range of the lexeme "righteousness." On the one hand, Irons considers arguments—and finds them lacking—that the "righteousness of God" is God's covenant faithfulness, or at the very least his saving activity or power. Consideration is given to significant texts such as Romans 1:16-17; 3:1-8, 25-26; and 2 Corinthians 5:21. On the other hand, Irons contends that seven out of the ten occurrences of the "righteousness of God" in Paul's literature refer to the gift of righteousness from God so that people receive a status as righteous before God by faith in Christ Jesus.[6]

## Convincing Arguments

As mentioned in the introduction, I find fundamental agreement with the thesis and argument of the book. Not surprisingly, then, in my estimation there are many more strengths than weaknesses in this book, and certainly more than I have space to mention. Nevertheless, I will focus on what I consider to be some of the strongest or most convincing arguments of the monograph.

### The Weight of Church History

As mentioned above, in Chapter 1 Irons demonstrates that the history of interpretation regarding the righteousness of God is remarkably consistent: the righteousness of God in Paul's letters is considered to be a gift—whether infused or imputed—to the individual. This consistency is found in both the Greek (e.g., Origen, Chrysostom) and Latin (e.g., Ambrosiaster, Augustine) fathers in the early church tradition; in the

---

6. The seven texts are: Rom 1:17; 3:21-22 (2x); 10:3 (2x); 2 Cor 5:21; and Phil 3:9. The other three are deemed examples of God's judging (or distributive) righteousness: Rom 3:5, 25-26

Medieval theologians (e.g., Peter Abelard, Thomas Aquinas); and in the Reformation and post-Reformation tradition (e.g., Martin Luther, Martin Bucer, John Calvin, William Perkins). Indeed, if Irons had broadened his survey to include all the righteousness terminology, it would have only strengthened his thesis, for as early as the 2nd century the tradition has a clear stream of interpretation in favor of righteousness as a gift.[7] If this survey is largely on point, then Irons has produced a rather potent argument for the traditional understanding of the righteousness of God and against the covenant faithfulness interpretation. Certainly it is true that the authority of a consistent stream of reception history does not outweigh the canonical authority of Scripture itself. Nevertheless, it is, generally speaking, a fool's errand to hold to an interpretation of Scripture that is relatively recent. At the very least, the burden of proof lies squarely on the new school of thought to prove the legitimacy of its interpretation.

## The Function of Hebrew Parallelism

One of the main arguments for the covenant faithfulness interpretation is that in the Old Testament—particularly in the Psalms and Isaiah—righteousness terminology is placed in parallel with terms such as "salvation" or "faithfulness."[8] It is assumed that "righteousness" therefore is synonymous with these parallel terms and thus should be understood as fundamentally a positive concept that describes God's commitment to bring "salvation" to his people in "faithfulness" to his covenant promises.

However, Irons demonstrates that this understanding of Hebrew parallelism is outdated and has been improved upon by a number of scholars, such as James Kugel, Robert Alter, and J. P. Fokkelman.[9] These scholars have rightly noted that "parallelism is almost never purely synonymous; rather, each line brings its own semantic contribution so that the sum is greater than the parts."[10] In other words, parallelism creates a surround sound stereo effect; when both terms are used in concert, they provide the reader with a fuller, richer, and deeper understanding of the concept. In the case of parallelism involving "righteousness" and "salvation," then, righteousness is "never purely synonymous" with "salvation." Rather, these two terms together connote a robust concept of God's saving righteousness whereby he delivers his people by means of judging his enemies.

A good example of this phenomenon is given regarding Isaiah 46:13.[11]

---

7. See, for instance, *1 Clement* 32.3-4; *Epistle to Diognetus* 9.1-6. For a thorough study of these and other texts, see Brian Arnold, *Justification in the Second Century* (Berlin: Walter de Gruyter, forthcoming).

8. See Psalms 40:10; 96:13; 143:1-2; Isa 45:8, 21; 46:12-13; 51:5-8.

9. Irons, *The Righteousness of God*, 66. See James L. Kugel, *The Idea of Biblical Poetry: Parallelism and Its History* (New Haven: Yale University Press, 1981); Robert Alter, *The Art of Biblical Poetry* (New York: Basic Books, 1985); J. P. Fokkelman, *Reading Biblical Poetry: An Introductory Guide*, trans. Ineke Smit (Louisville: WJK, 2001).

10. Irons, *The Righteousness of God*, 143.

11. Ibid., 147.

> I am bringing my <u>righteousness</u> near,
>> it is not far away;
>> and my <u>salvation</u> will not be delayed.
> I will grant <u>salvation</u> to Zion,
>> my <u>splendor</u> to Israel (NIV).

In this text "righteousness" is parallel with "salvation," and "salvation" with "splendor." As Irons rightly notes, it is unlikely that "salvation" and "splendor" are pure synonyms, and therefore "salvation" and "righteousness" are not pure synonyms either. Rather, each term adds a new perspective on what God will do to save his people: "it is a salvation that (a) comes by means of his righteous judicial activity and (b) results in splendor or glory."[12] In other words, "righteousness" does not *mean* salvation any more than "salvation" *means* "righteousness." To define it as such is to strip the parallelism of its surround sound stereo effect.

## The Righteousness of God as the Righteousness of Faith in Romans 3:21-22

Another convincing argument is that at least seven of the ten occurrences of the phrase "righteousness of God" in Paul's letters are equated with the righteousness of faith, and that therefore the righteousness of God is a gift of divinely-approved righteousness from God. For the sake of space I would like to focus particularly on Irons' analysis of Romans 3:21-22, a hotly debated and climactic paragraph regarding God's righteousness, and provide additional analysis for support.

From Romans 1:18-3:20 Paul demonstrated that "everyone, both Jew and Gentile, is under sin" (3:9), that "there is no one righteous" (3:10), and that therefore "by the works of the law no flesh will be justified before him" (3:20). In 3:21 Paul asserts that there is a divine solution to the plight of humanity: "But now apart from the law the righteousness of God has been manifested." The phrase "righteousness of God" hearkens back to the thesis of the letter, which asserts that the reason the gospel is powerful to save is "because in it is revealed the righteousness of God" (1:16-17).

The question is, what exactly is the "righteousness of God," and why is it the solution to humanity's plight? Some commentators have understood the phrase to refer to God's saving activity in fulfillment of his covenant promises. While this is possible, more likely God's righteousness refers to the righteousness he gives to all those who have faith in Christ. First, the righteousness of God in 3:21 is immediately

---

12. Ibid.

qualified in 3:22 as that which is "by faith in Jesus Christ" and "for all who believe."[13] The emphasis on a righteousness "by faith" indicates that the righteousness in view is something that is *received by* individuals, not merely something *performed for the sake of* individuals. In other words, the righteousness of God is equated with the righteousness of faith. The former emphasizes the divine source of righteousness, whereas the latter the means by which individuals receive righteousness.

Second, 3:21-22 finds a verbal parallel in 3:24, where believers are "declared righteous" by God through Christ.[14] The structure of the paragraph is as follows:

Righteousness of God (3:21-26)
Negative means of righteousness: manifested apart from the law (3:21)
Positive means of righteousness: received by faith in Jesus Christ (3:22)
Parenthesis (3:23)
Basis of righteousness (3:24-26)

In 3:21 the righteousness of God is defined negatively (as something manifested "apart from the law"), and in 3:22a it is defined positively (as something received by faith and given to anyone who believes). Verses 22b-23 form a parenthesis explaining why both Jews and Gentiles can access this righteousness by faith alone. Then in 3:24-26 Paul explains the basis for this gift of righteousness: it comes to individuals "freely by his grace" (3:24a) and is rooted in the redemptive and propitiatory sacrifice of Christ (3:24b-25a). Because of Christ's death, God is proven to be "just and the justifier of the one who has faith in Jesus" (3:26).[15] The gift-character of this righteousness is especially clear in that individuals who receive the righteousness of God by faith (3:22)

---

13. Regarding the πίστις Χριστοῦ ("faith of Christ") debate, Irons adheres (ibid., 329-34) to the objective genitive ("faith in Christ") as opposed to the subjective genitive ("faithfulness of Christ"). It is sometimes averred that the phrase διὰ πίστεως Ἰησοῦ Χριστοῦ ("through the faith of Jesus Christ") in Rom 3:22 must refer to Jesus' own faithfulness as the means of God's righteousness, for otherwise the phrase "for all who believe" would be redundant. If this is the case, then it is thought that the righteousness of God would naturally refer to God's saving activity enacted for believers by means of the faithfulness of Jesus, particularly in his death and resurrection. With Irons, my sympathies lie with the objective genitive view, and I agree with Irons on 3:22: "Paul wants to make two points about the role of faith in appropriating this righteousness: it is received by faith, and it comes to all who believe, whether Jew or Gentile" (ibid., 322). Nevertheless, unlike Irons, I do not think the subjective genitive interpretation would "seriously undercut" the argument (ibid., 329), for Paul would merely be emphasizing that the righteousness-before God that is "for all who believe" is provided by means of Jesus' faithful life, death, and resurrection.

14. Ibid., 323. At this point translations may obscure the lexical connection between 3:21-22 and 3:24. The noun δικαιοσύνη appears in the former, and the passive participle of the verb δικαιόω ("to declare righteous") in the latter.

15. With Irons (ibid., 279-89), the last two occurrences of the "righteousness of God" in 3:25-26 likely refer to God's distributive justice (cf. 3:5). Irons' analysis of the meaning of πάρεσις and ἔνδειξις is especially sound: he argues that πάρεσις describes God "passing over sins" (as opposed to "forgiving sins"), and that ἔνδειξις has to do with God "demonstrating" (as opposed to "displaying") his righteousness.

are "declared righteous" (δικαιούμενοι) by God—that is, given a status of "righteous" (3:24).[16]

Third, Irons follows and builds upon the argument of Thomas R. Schreiner in recognizing the close parallels between Romans 3:21-22; 10:3; and Philippians 3:9.[17] In Romans 10:3, Paul attests that Israel did not submit to the righteousness of God but rather sought to establish their own righteousness. In the near context (9:30-10:13), Israel's pursuit of self-righteousness is described as a pursuit of a "law of righteousness" (9:31; cf. 10:5), whereas the Gentiles, who were not pursuing righteousness, obtained the "righteousness of faith" (9:30; cf. 10:6). Given the immediate context of Romans 10:3, it appears that the righteousness of God is equated with the righteousness of faith, and self-righteousness is equated with the righteousness of the law.

In Philippians 3:9, Paul rejects as loss "my own righteousness that is from the law" but instead finds of surpassing value a "righteousness through faith in Christ," which explicitly is defined as a "righteousness from (ἐκ) God." One would be hard-pressed to miss the gift-character of the righteousness of God in this text!

The remarkable parallels between Romans 10:3 and Philippians 3:9 make it likely that the "righteousness of God" and the "righteousness of faith" refer to the same righteousness, namely, an individual's divinely-given and divinely-approved righteousness before God.[18] Moreover, since Romans 3:21-22 (cf. 1:16-17) is itself parallel to 10:3, it is likely that even in 1:16-17 and 3:21-22 the same conclusion obtains regarding the nature of the righteousness of God.

## God's Righteousness as the Basis for His Covenant Faithfulness

One of the shortcomings of the book is that it underestimates the pervasiveness of the covenant theme in Scripture. Irons is (rightly) concerned that interpreters can too easily let the covenant motif overpower the lexical data of any given text.[19] But there is also the danger of going too far in the other direction, so as to effectively mute the covenantal theme when present. Even though I agree that at the lexical level righteousness does not mean covenant faithfulness, at the discourse level righteousness may occur in more covenantal contexts than Irons allows.

For example, Irons claims of Isaiah 45:21, "Nothing in the context suggests that 'a righteous God' is code for God's covenant faithfulness to Israel, a thought that would

---

16. Irons also notes that righteousness in Romans is called a "free gift" in Rom 5:17 and 6:23, suggesting the gift-character of righteousness (ibid., 316-17).

17. Ibid., 334-36. Schreiner's argument appears in *New Testament Theology: Magnifying God in Christ* (Grand Rapids: Baker Academic, 2008), 357-58.

18. Those who dismiss the parallels with Phil 3:9 because they are not exact either unduly require rigidity in Greek syntax (especially regarding the use of prepositions) or wrongly assume that the phrase "righteousness of God" is a *terminus technicus*. On this last point, see Irons' insightful critique of Ernst Käsemann and Peter Stuhlmacher (ibid., 41-48).

19. See his insightful critique of N. T. Wright on this point (ibid., 113 n.11).

be out of place in the immediate context, which is a polemic against Gentile idolatry and a universal call to all the nations to acknowledge the one true God."[20] In reality, though, the immediate context of the call for the nations to leave their idols is promissory: the nations will come to Zion (45:14) and will turn and be saved, and they will confess that Yahweh is their God (45:23). These promises are thoroughly covenantal, for they are rooted in the worldwide promises to Abraham (e.g., Gen 12:3) and David (2 Sam 7:19; Psa 72:8-11, 17). Hence, even though I agree with Irons that the phrase "a righteous God" (Isa 45:21) is not a cipher for God's covenant faithfulness in the lexical level, at the discourse level God's righteousness that is received by all the people of God (45:24-25) fulfills his covenant promises to Abraham and David.

A similar example comes from Irons' analysis of some of the messianic texts in Isaiah (11:1-5; 16:5; 42:3-4).[21] Regarding the work of the Servant of Yahweh in 42:3-4 he claims "It has nothing to do with keeping one's promises, i.e., covenant faithfulness."[22] But surely this is an overstatement, for the promise of a future Davidic king is rooted in God's promises to David (2 Sam 7:11-16).[23] Furthermore, Isaiah 42:4 asserts that "the coastlands wait for his law." The word "law" refers to the Torah or the instruction of the king, which echoes the promise of 2 Samuel 7:19 that the covenant with David would be "the Torah for humanity" (cf. Isa 2:3).[24] Finally, this future king will rule in covenantally faithful ways, for his rule is characterized by faithfulness to the Torah. In 16:5, for instance, Isaiah uses two word pairs that summarize the covenant relationship and responsibilities of the king. On the one hand, he will rule will "steadfast love" (חֶסֶד) and "faithfulness" (אֱמֶת), which summarize the king's covenant relationship with God and the people. On the other hand, he will rule with "justice" (מִשְׁפָּט) and "righteousness" (צֶדֶק), which summarize the king's covenant responsibilities toward God and the people. In other words, the king will model for the people covenant faithfulness, as outlined in Deuteronomy 17:18-20.[25] Isaiah's hope for a future king, then, is rooted in covenantal language. Again, this does not entail that "righteousness" *means*

---

20. Ibid., 146. See also Irons' overstatement regarding Isa 46:12-13, "Righteousness here is certainly not God's covenant faithfulness, a thought that is totally foreign to the context" (ibid., 148).

21. Ibid., 152-53.

22. Ibid., 153.

23. It is likely that the Servant of Yahweh in Isaiah is a king (John T. Willis, *Isaiah*, The Living Word Commentary on the Old Testament [Austin, TX: Sweet, 1980], 421; contra Christopher R. North, *The Suffering Servant in Deutero-Isaiah: An Historical and Critical Study* [London: Oxford University Press, 1948]); cf. Isa 11:1; 53:2; 55:3.

24. For excellent analyses of 2 Sam 7:19, see Walter C. Kaiser, Jr., "The Blessing of David: The Charter for Humanity," in *The Law and the Prophets: Old Testament Studies Prepared in Honor of Oswald Thompson Allis*, ed. John H. Skilton (Philadelphia: Presbyterian and Reformed, 1974), 298-318; Peter J. Gentry and Stephen J. Wellum, *Kingdom through Covenant: A Biblical-Theological Understanding of the Covenants* (Wheaton, IL: Crossway, 2012), 399-400.

25. For a more extended treatment of Isaiah's word pairs, see Thomas L. Leclerc, *Yahweh Is Exalted in Justice: Solidarity and Conflict in Isaiah* (Minneapolis: Fortress, 2001); Gentry and Wellum, *Kingdom through Covenant*, 577-82.

"covenant faithfulness," but rather that God's righteousness and the righteousness of the future king fulfill God's promises to David.

To be clear, righteousness terminology is not always used in covenantal contexts; indeed, regarding righteousness terminology in the Hebrew Scripture, Irons notes that such language is "'profiled' against 'the base' of the judicial setting rather than the covenantal setting."[26] Still, Irons doesn't sufficiently take into account how pervasive the covenant concept is in Scripture, even where the word "covenant" does not appear.

It would strengthen Irons' thesis to show more clearly that God's righteousness in Scripture is tied closely to God's covenant faithfulness in that the former is the basis for the latter. Nehemiah 9:8 shows this relationship most clearly: "You found [Abraham's] heart faithful before you, and made with him the covenant to give to his offspring the land of the Canaanite, the Hittite, the Amorite, the Perizzite, the Jebusite, and the Girgashite. And you have kept your promise, for you are righteous" (ESV).[27] The basis for God's covenant-keeping shown to Abraham is God's righteous character (note: "*for* you are righteous"). Irons recognizes this relationship implicitly at points in his argument, for he approvingly quotes Mark A. Seifrid a number of times in the book: "all 'covenant-keeping' is righteous behavior, but not all righteous behavior is 'covenant-keeping.'"[28] This quote is intended to show a distinction between righteousness and covenant faithfulness, but at the same time it also (rightly) asserts that covenant-keeping is a subset or a function of righteousness.[29] Hence, God's righteousness is the basis for his covenant-keeping, and our divinely-approved righteousness before God is the basis for our covenant-keeping as well. This is not to say that God's righteousness is *equated* with his "covenant faithfulness," nor that justification in Paul's theology *means* "covenant membership." Rather, God keeps his covenant promises *because* he is righteous, and Christians are reconciled to God in a new covenant relationship through Christ *because* of the gift of a divinely-approved righteousness (see

---

26. Irons, *The Righteousness of God*, 125. Even though it needs minor alteration, the evidence provided by Mark A. Seifrid regarding how infrequently covenant and righteousness terminology overlap is weighty and should not be ignored (Mark A. Seifrid, "Righteousness Language in the Hebrew Scriptures and Early Judaism," in *Justification and Variegated Nomism, Vol. 1: The Complexities of Second Temple Judaism*, Wissenschaftliche Untersuchungen zum Neuen Testament 2/140, ed. D. A. Carson, Peter T. O'Brien, and Mark A. Seifrid [Tübingen: Mohr Siebeck/Grand Rapids: Baker Academic, 2001], 423 [as cited in Irons, *The Righteousness of God*, 126 n.28]). Also salient is Irons' comment (*The Righteousness of God*, 296) that Paul's "righteousness of God" terminology does not occur adjacent to his "promise" terminology.

27. Irons mentions Nehemiah 9:8 twice (ibid., 136 n.71, 154 n.97).

28. Seifrid, "Righteousness Language in the Hebrew Scriptures," 424 (as cited in Irons, *The Righteousness of God*, 106 n.93, 136 n.71, 143, 154 n.97).

29. Irons actually recognizes that "keeping one's promises is a subset of righteousness" (*The Righteousness of God*, 154 n.97), and that "God's saving activity comes in fulfillment of his covenant promises and is an expression of his righteousness" (156). But his view needs to be more clearly differentiated from that Irons' main interlocutor Hermann Cremer, who also argues that God's righteousness fulfills his covenant promises (see esp. ibid., 35, 133-34).

Rom 5:1; 2 Cor 5:18-21).[30] This explanation of the relationship between righteousness and covenant faithfulness maintains a right balance, for on the one hand it guards the lexical distinction between the terminologies, and on the other it makes sense of the interplay between both concepts that are pervasive in Scripture.

## Concluding Thoughts

In *The Righteousness of God*, Irons has provided what is now the definitive lexical study of the phrase "righteousness of God" in Paul's letters. The argument of the book is, if anything, inextricably lexical in nature, and at this point it succeeds in divorcing "covenant faithfulness" from the meaning of righteousness. Any future treatment of Paul's understanding of God's righteousness or the meaning of righteousness terminology in Scripture must reckon with the thesis and argument of this monograph.

### Areas for Future Research

With this in mind, I would like to suggest two areas for future research. First, what role do principles of noun formation play in determining lexical semantics? In particular, the Greek noun ending –συνη connotes a character quality or attribute, suggesting that the term δικαιοσύνη ("righteousness") has to do with the "quality" or "attribute" of δίκαιος ("righteous") applied to an individual. If this is the case, how does this affect the meaning of δικαιοσύνη in its various contexts? Is it proper to speak of, say, a subjective or objective genitive of a noun that isn't inherently verbal in nature?

Second, Irons rightly asserts that the way in which we enjoy the gift of God's righteousness comes by our union with Christ; that is, we receive a righteousness imputed to us by faith in Christ.[31] But how precisely are we to understand the nature of our union with Christ, and how do corporate and representative notions of kingship in the ancient world help us think through the nature of the "sweet exchange" of our sin for Christ's righteousness? Also, what precisely do we mean by the term "imputed"? Can we speak of a righteousness "earned" or "merited" for us by Christ?

### Why Does This Matter?

In closing, why does it matter that we understand aright the meaning of the "righteousness of God"? First—and perhaps most obviously—a *lexical study* of God's righteousness ultimately has to do with a *theological study* of God's righteousness. Regarding Hermann Cremer's claim that righteousness is "thoroughly positive," Irons insightfully comments, "At its base, this is much more than a lexical claim; it

---

30. See Irons' good analysis of the relationship between justification and reconciliation (ibid., 341-42).

31. Ibid., 328.

is a theological claim about the very concept of 'righteousness' in biblical theology."[32] More specifically, Irons concludes that if Cremer's view of righteousness is correct, "then this is simply the end of the concept of God's distributive justice."[33] In other words, lexical semantics is foundational for theology!

Finally, the reason why this issue should be taken seriously is that it has everything to do with how an individual can be assured of final justification. If, as some have argued, righteousness and justification do not have so much to do with soteriology (how a person gets saved) as much as with ecclesiology (who a person can have table fellowship with), then what is the basis for the Christian's soteriological hope on the last day? If, however, "justification is a matter of how sinful humans can be righteous before the divine tribunal,"[34] then it has everything to do with a person's assurance of final justification. Ultimately, the basis for our assurance that our new covenant relationship with God is real and never-ending is Jesus' propitiatory death, which pays the penalty of our sin and brings us the gift of righteousness before God (see Rom 5:1). This righteousness alone, like Luther came to understand and embrace, is "the gate to paradise."

---

32. Ibid., 134.
33. Ibid., 340.
34. Ibid., 342.

# A Critical Review of Charles Lee Irons' *The Righteousness of God*

Irons, Charles Lee. *The Righteousness of God: A Lexical Examination of the Covenant-Faithfulness Interpretation*. Wissenschaftliche Untersuchungen zum Neuen Testament 2/386. Tübingen: Mohr Siebeck, 2015. 444 pp.

## John Frederick

John Frederick has a PhD in New Testament and teaches New Testament, theology, and worship arts at Grand Canyon University. He is a priest in the Anglican Church in North America and serves at Christus Victor Anglican Church in Phoenix, AZ.

### Introduction

Charles Lee Irons' 2015 Mohr Siebeck monograph entitled, *The Righteousness of God*, is an admirable work of serious New Testament scholarship focusing on the usage of the Greek phrase *dikaiosunē Theou* ("the righteousness of God") in its Jewish, Greco-Roman, and canonical attestations. The book contributes valuable new research on the phrase 'the righteousness of God' and contains an exhaustive survey of the history of interpretation of the biblical texts that use the phrase (ch.1). After setting the stage with methodological considerations in chapter 2, Irons embarks on the main portion of the work, namely a lexical study of the extra-biblical Greek sources (ch.3), the Old Testament sources (ch.4), and the extra-biblical apocryphal and pseudepigraphal Jewish sources (ch.5). The book concludes with a comparative of study of the usage of the term in the epistles of Paul (ch.6), a synopsis (ch.7), and a comprehensive, 38-page appendix which lists and categorizes all of the occurrences of the word 'righteousness' in the Old Testament.

The purpose of the monograph, according to Irons, is to undermine the relational view of the word 'righteousness' which, he argues, the New Perspective on Paul has viewed as a "cipher" for "inappropriate covenantal categories." These covenantal categories, he argues, have contributed to the adoption of a skewed understanding of Paul's doctrine of justification which departs from the history of interpretation of the phrase "the righteousness of God" and abandons the Reformation-era understanding of the forensic imputation of "righteousness" as the proper focal point of the doctrine of justification. From this error Irons desires to "rescue" the doctrine of justification from out of the hands of adherents of the New Perspective by highlighting the "fallacious" root of that view in the writings of Hermann Cremer.[1]

Irons' thesis maintains that Cremer's early works have introduced a faulty understanding of 'righteousness' as a relational term, emphasizing right covenant relationship with God. This view, he argues, has contributed to the rejection in New Testament studies of Lutheran ideas of imputation and other primarily judicial understandings of the doctrine. Indeed, in chapter 1 Irons pronounces his desire "to undermine the central lexical basis of the New Perspective interpretation of 'the righteousness of God'" in order to "vindicate" the Old Lutheran perspective on Paul. In a moment of personal affirmation he declares in his concluding chapter (ch.7) that he has, in fact, successfully undermined the New Perspective in his monograph. However, I cannot join Irons in his assessment of his monograph's success in vindicating the Old Perspective view of justification. Rather, I find his thesis to falter in regard to the stated goal of undermining the New Perspective on Paul. I will approach the critique of the monograph in three movements, namely: (1) a critique of Irons' methodological approach, (2) a critique of Irons' view of 'righteousness' as a non-covenantal, judicial/forensic term and category, and (3) a critique of Irons' view of Judaism.

## A Critique of Irons' Lexical Approach: The Necessity of Context for the Determination of the Theological Function of a Word

Central to Irons' project is a methodological approach which seeks to determine the proper theological meaning of 'the righteousness of God' via a lexical study of the phrase in various literary works from antiquity. His monograph is essentially a word study that surveys the usage of the terms in a variety of sources, and then categorizes their uses into a list that expresses the basic semantic field of possible meanings of the word(s). As can be observed in the appendix (p. 344), Irons enumerates three key domains of usage for the term "righteousness," namely: legal righteousness (i.e., courtroom language), ethical righteousness, and correctness (i.e., speaking the truth, using just balances, etc). It must be stated that in terms of exhaustive lexical comparative work, the monograph is exemplary in regard to its breadth and in regard to the author's ability to organize the results into a useful scholarly resource. In chapters 1-5, Irons' command of the material, and his concise, informative summaries of the various authors and works stand on their own as useful overviews of often obscure texts. The worth of these chapters is evident quite apart from any potential contribution they are intended to make toward the establishment of the monograph's main thesis. In terms of lexical study Irons proves himself to be a master of the task.

---

1. Charles Lee Irons, *The Righteousness of God: A Lexical Examination of the Covenant-Faithfulness Interpretation*, Wissenschaftliche Untersuchungen zum Neuen Testament 2/386 (Tübingen: Mohr Siebeck, 2015), 6-7.

Yet, where I find fault with this type of lexical approach is in the primacy of place it gives to the meaning of words above, and in some cases instead of, the determination of the theological function of a phrase in its theological context. The decision to approach the task in this manner is overt. When Irons states that his word-study approach is undertaken *instead of* an engagement with "the broad brush of *theological* motifs," it becomes evident that too much autonomy and weight is being given to words and phrases apart from their *particular* uses in *particular* New Testament texts to express *particular* theological emphases and fulfilling *particular* theological functions. Irons frequently re-presents this primary methodological prolegomena whereby a focus on the meaning of the phrase 'righteousness of God' seems to operate in a Platonic manner in which a generic meaning determined from the semantic field of possible meanings governs and restricts how the word is allowed to operate in any given *theological* context. This problematic approach can be observed when Irons insists that the early church fathers understood the phrase "righteousness of God" not in an "esoteric Hebraic/relational sense that bears no relationship to what the word actually means in Greek" but rather in a sense "that was consistent with *the ordinary meanings* associated with the Greek word *dikaiosunē*."[2] Elsewhere Irons argues in a similar manner that New Perspective scholars have introduced the meaning "covenant faithfulness" into the *dik-* word group.[3] Irons states overtly that: "the contextual concept must not be equated with the lexical concept"[4] and that, although the word "righteousness" *can* be used "to refer to faithfulness," nevertheless, "faithfulness is not part of *the lexical sense*" of the word "righteous."[5] Indeed, Irons goes so far as to say that the "*discourse concepts* in the surrounding context should not be allowed to *overpower the lexical concepts of the world themselves.*"[6] For Irons, Paul is "tethered" to the results of the range of lexical options that arise from the study of the usage of the word in the biblical and non-biblical works in antiquity. This approach does not sufficiently take into account the way in which words take on *a specific theological function* in its immediate context; a function that is not discernible from the mere study of the semantic domain of a lexeme in a generic, blanket fashion across a sampling of disparate, decontexualized, and disconnected texts.[7] Instead, as Irons himself recognizes, even if the word "righteousness" does not literally mean "covenant faithfulness" in a "lexical sense" it can be and is used in both biblical and extra-biblical

2. Ibid., 5. Emphasis mine.
3. Ibid., 83.
4. Ibid., 88
5. Ibid., 89. Emphasis mine.
6. Ibid., 150. Emphasis mine.
7. Ibid. 273. Irons makes a concession here by noting that it is possible that Paul could transform "the linguistic usage" of a word, thus creating a new sort of meaning. Although, he has already conveniently noted on the previous page (p. 272) that the meaning "covenant faithfulness" does not fit this category of "transformed meaning."

Greek "with reference to covenant relationships."[8] This demonstrates that even if one prefers to approach the "meaning" of a word apart from its actual usage in a particular discourse, the word will end up being defined in much greater detail when it is read within the actual context of the discourse in which it is being used. Therefore, while a lexical study many be interesting, and helpful for the generic formation of a lexicon entry, it is utterly useless as an exegetical tool unless it is considered in tandem with the theological function of the word within a given discourse. Such a methodological oversight invites skewed results and, instead of undermining the New Perspective, undermines Irons' entire project.

In regard to the approach of Irons' project, there are two additional points of his methodology that need to be addressed, namely: (1) his use of a semantic domain comparison which I find to be rigged and which issues forth in unreliable and warped conclusions, and (2) the liberty with which he reads his own theological presuppositions into the exegetical process. We shall conclude this section by briefly addressing each of these critiques before moving on to assess his arguments in regard to "righteousness" in the monograph.

Concerning Irons' use of a semantic domain comparison, he explains on p. 109:

> In addition to examining the semantic range of the words for 'righteousness,' I also compare these words with other words in two semantic domains, 'courts and legal procedures' and 'moral and ethical qualities.' As we will see, this semantic domain analysis goes a long way toward clarifying the precise contours of the semantic profile of the words for 'righteousness' and the particular social context that they presuppose.[9]

Although there is much value in performing a comparative (in addition to a lexical) semantic domain analysis, the problem with Irons' use of this procedure is that it essentially assumes in advance that any view of "righteousness" defined in relational and/or covenantal terms is by default ruled out. By selecting only two domains of meaning, namely legal and ethical usages of the term, the domain of covenantal/relational "righteousness" is decidedly not represented. Therefore, the conclusions of the comparative study really offer no additional information about the possibility of a covenantal or relational view of "righteousness" because Irons' did not include that category within his comparative search. That is to say, Irons pre-determined set of lexical categories for the semantic possibilities of the word 'righteousness'(namely: legal, ethical, and correctness categories) necessarily govern the semantic comparison, and this forces the study to ignore potentially illuminating instances of words that refer to faithfulness to a contract, agreement, or covenant.

---

8. Ibid., 90. Cf. 105 in which Irons notes that it can be shown extra-biblical Greek documents that the word *dikaiosunē* ("righteousness") can refer to "social relationships [that] are formalized as promises, oaths, contracts, covenants, treaties, and so on"; cf. 151.

9. Ibid., 109.

This same commitment to predetermined ideas is evident in Irons' theological presuppositions which are rooted in the Reformed tradition. It is, no doubt, impossible for any interpreter to be entirely objective. Likewise, it is well-known that no interpreter can escape the reality of the theory-laden nature of all knowledge. Our ideas and commitments remain with us even when we are trying to remain 'neutral.' Thus, I am not critiquing Irons for holding firm to his faith commitments as an exegete. On the contrary, I commend such a commitment to a pious adherence to one's faith tradition within the fabric of Christian orthodoxy. However, I find an unacceptable level of cross-over of Irons' theological positions—which themselves are reliant to some extent on the exegesis of Scripture—into his exegetical work. When Irons rattles off theological terms and doctrinal positions such as the distinction between "justification and sanctification," and the reality of "human inability and sovereign grace"[10] his comments reveal his commitment to Reformed theological presuppositions which contribute to his own inability and unwillingness to accommodate the findings of the New Perspective in regard to "righteousness" into his theological system. Perhaps this is one of the reasons that he desires to "rescue" biblical studies by "undermining" an alleged erroneous New Perspective interpretation of the doctrine of justification.[11] Lest one think that I am overstating my case, further comments about "the Pauline doctrine of grace," the reality of "sovereign grace,"[12] and a "monergistic accent . . . manifested in the salvation and conversion of the elect"[13] further demonstrate Irons' tendency to approach exegesis from an overly dogmatic perspective. The critique here is not that Irons' attempted to do theology, so to speak, but rather that his weaving in and out of the exegetical and theological tasks is not cohesive with the rest of his project, and lacks the precision and care that is evidenced in his earlier, lexical work. Nor is my issue here with Irons' theological ideas per se. Rather, my critique is more specifically directed at the fact that his exegetical points from New Testament texts do not obviously issue forth in the sort of grand theological ideas that he assumes in an obvious and uncontested fashion. That is to say, not all interpreters would agree on the theological take-aways from an exegesis of the passages treated by Irons. Thus, his theological presuppositions cannot be used to function as evidence for his theory about "righteousness" contra the New Perspective without a much more extensive theological and exegetical treatment of the individual New Testament texts.

---

10. Ibid., 294. Cf. p. 292 where he refers to the concept of "union with Christ" without establishing or even defining what he means by that. I am not opposed to these ideas at all. Rather, I aim to highlight the fact that melding such theological presuppositions into a section on exegesis is methodologically improper.

11. Ibid., 6-7.

12. Ibid., 294. The "doctrines of grace" is a phrase that is commonly used synonymously with Reformed Theology and Calvinism.

13. Ibid., 318.

## A Critique of Irons' View of "Righteousness" as a Non-Covenantal, Judicial/Forensic Term and Category

On the topic of "righteousness" Irons makes a solid and convincing case against Hermann Cremer's view that "righteousness" is primarily a positive concept, referring not to distributive justice and the divine response to legal realities in regard to humans, but rather referring to one's positive relationship with God.[14] Irons' next move is to demonstrate through a lexical study that the word "righteousness" (a) never means "covenant-faithfulness" as it is often translated by adherents of the New Perspective, and (b) refers primarily to the forensic dealings of God with humanity according to the principle of justice which corresponds and coheres with God's perfectly just character. Further, it is a main contention of Irons' that by undermining the relational view of Cremer, he has undermined the entire New Perspective position. Though I do not take issue, and on the contrary, agree with Irons' critique of Cremer's solely positive view of God's righteousness, I do take issue with virtually all of the conclusions that he draws from this fact.

To begin, it is not the case that a successful critique of Cremer's position on "righteousness" thereby undermines the New Perspective.[15] A successful critique of Cremer *does* calls into question *Cremer's* theology. Yet, the various views of the adherents of the variegated movement known as the New Perspective on Paul cannot simply be dismissed because of an inconsistency in Cremer's exegesis and theology. After all, Cremer was a thinker who *preceded* the New Perspective. If one wants to critique, for example, N.T. Wright, in what way does it make sense to do this by critiquing a scholar who is not cited, quoted, or included in any book or bibliography by Wright? A quick look through all of N.T. Wright's major works reveals that Cremer is never even mentioned! Thus, it would require a massive, improbable stretch to conclude that Cremer's ideas provide the main foundation for Wright's theology of 'righteousness.' Would it not make more sense, if one is seeking to undermine the New Perspective—a movement to which Cremer never even belonged—to perhaps critique its leading exponents, namely James D.G. Dunn and N.T .Wright? To be fair, Irons does establish the positive influence of Cremer on Dunn via his usage of Achtemeier's *The Interpreters Dictionary of the Bible,* a source indebted to the work of Cremer and a source which Dunn cites.[16] Yet, even this example occupies a tiny portion of the monograph, perhaps a few sentences, and is, at best, a piece of circumstantial and indirect evidence. If Irons actually wanted to say something about the effect of his monograph on the New Perspectives of Dunn and Wright, he ought to have engaged directly with their

---

14. Cf. Ibid., 182: "Cremer's analysis failed to take account of the bi-directional flow of God's righteousness, that is, the fact that God is described as 'a righteous judge' because he righteously defends the innocent and punishes their oppressors"; cf. 134-135. I complete agree with this assessment and I find it to be a valuable contribution to the scholarly discussion.

15. Ibid., 10.

16. Ibid., 37.

works which, I would argue, are based not on the slavish adoption of an idea from one scholar (namely Cremer), but are part of a wide interpretive movement in biblical scholarship and which—in any case—make their own arguments for the covenantal reading of *dikaiosunē*. The most egregious error in this regard, however, comes from the relegating of the findings and formulations of Wright's latest work on Paul and justification to a handful of minor footnotes. This oversight allows Irons to construct a strawman which attributes to Wright a sort of monolithic view of "righteousness" that is basically equivalent to Cremer and refers to "righteousness" solely as "covenant faithfulness" apart from judicial overtones. What is most surprising about this is that Irons actually reveals early on in the book that he knows that this truncated understanding of "righteousness" is actually not what Wright argues for in his latest book! On page 58, buried in footnote 220, Irons notes that, in fact, in Wright's book, *Paul and the Faithfulness of God*,[17] he argues not for a monolithic, but rather for a four-fold sense to "righteousness" which includes "right behavior, the law court, the covenant, and eschatological cosmic rectification."[18] Thus, while it would be correct to conclude that Irons' project has succeeded in critiquing the exegesis of Hermann Cremer, the lack of Wright's use of Cremer and Wright's four-fold sense of "righteousness" makes any claim by Irons' to have defeated a *Wrightian* account of the New Perspective severely inaccurate. Related to and exacerbating this error is Irons' own admission that though, in regard to the lexeme itself, the word "righteousness" does not mean "covenant faithfulness," nevertheless, as was stated earlier, the word *dikaiosunē* ("righteousness") can be used to refer to faithfulness to a contract, agreement or promise.[19] In his discussion of parallelism in Isa 56:1; Ps 36:10; Ps 143:1, Irons argues:

> God's 'righteousness' includes his being faithful to keep his promises and deliver his people. But this does not mean that the word 'righteousness' means faithfulness to a promissory covenant. All instances of faithfulness to a promissory covenant may be termed 'righteousness,' but not all 'righteousness' is faithfulness to a promissory covenant.[20]

Thus, in stating that instances of faithfulness to a covenant can be referred to as "righteousness," Irons is unknowingly conceding a major point to the New Perspective. The New Perspective understanding of "righteousness" as a status of right covenantal relationship with God on the basis of the faithfulness of Jesus Christ to all who have the covenant badge of faith relies not on the meaning of a mere lexeme determined without reference to its usage in a particular text and detached from its immediate literary context. Instead, the New Perspective approach focuses on the theological function of the lexeme "righteousness" and the phrase "the righteousness of God"

---

17. N.T. Wright, *Paul and the Faithfulness of God*, 2 vols. (Minneapolis: Fortress, 2013).
18. Ibid., 58 n.220. Emphasis mine.
19. Ibid., 105, citing this usage in Dionysius of Halicarnassus, *Ant. Rom.* 2.75.1.
20. Ibid., 143.

(and their related variations) in their particular Pauline contexts. It is, therefore, a moot point, to quibble over the semantic domain of a word, and to make theological arguments on that basis when the context has been purposefully ignored.

This mishmash of misrepresentations and strawman arguments in regard to N.T. Wright's true understanding of the function of the *dik-* ("righteousness") word group leads to a subsequent simplification of "righteousness" by Irons that, in shutting out any covenantal and relational meaning in advance, relegates the term to a primarily forensic, legal function. But we have already observed in the most recent writings of New Perspective advocate N.T. Wright, that the forensic/legal language of the court room need not, and indeed should not, be separated from the covenantal, cosmic-eschatological, and ethical nuances of the word *dikaiosunē*. Indeed, to exclude the category of "covenant" from one's understanding of divine justice is to decontextualize the mechanism by which the concept of divine justice makes any canonical sense in the first place, namely within the context of a covenant relationship with God, either as a covenant-keeper or a covenant-breaker. In order to downplay, or even to reject the covenantal context and the covenantal nature of divine court-room language in the Bible, one must abstract the notion of justice from the very paradigm in which it find its coherence. Divine justice in regard to Israel is always a *covenantal* justice. Thus, the most notable misstep of Irons is his decovenantalizing of "righteousness" and divine justice.

Irons' notes, for example, that the Old Testament words for "righteous/righteousness" often refer to judicial, legal situations *within the people of Israel*. Yet, he then immediately critiques Wright by arguing that Wright:

> ties the law-court imagery too closely to the Abrahamic covenant, and in fact makes the covenant the primary category for interpreting the righteousness language…the forensic character of God's righteousness is muted and the phrase ultimately becomes a cipher for God's faithfulness to his covenant. Once the overpowering covenant motif is removed from Wright's construction, much of what he says about the Hebrew law court is helpful and valid.[21]

Why, though, must the law court metaphor be removed from and abstracted from its inseparable covenant context? This makes no sense and should be considered an exegetical error and oversight. Even referring to the concept of "righteousness" within "Israel" itself necessitates a reference to the covenant, the Torah which functions as the guiding legal document that provides the context and ground for understanding the justice of God in relation to his people and to those who are outside of the covenant community. This position frequently reoccurs throughout the monograph. Elsewhere Irons contrasts covenant themes with forensic themes in a similarly binary and polar

---

21. Ibid., 113. This is another example, by the way, of Irons' use of an older, popular level text by Wright instead of engaging with his newest, academic magnum opus on Paul. In this case, *What Saint Paul Really Said: Was Paul of Tarsus the Real Founder of Christianity?* (Grand Rapids: Eerdmans, 1997).

fashion, indicating that "righteousness words" have their "'base,' 'frame,' and 'social setting'" in the language of the judicial court *rather than* the covenant.[22] Similarly, even *salvation itself*, Irons argues, "is an essentially judicial activity."[23]

Thus, given the critiques above, it must be stated that Irons' own understanding of "righteousness" as a purely forensic, non-covenantal reality is, in fact, a result of an error which he ironically attributes to the various adherents of the New Perspective, namely, the importing of an incomplete, incorrect understanding of "righteousness" into the biblical and theological function of the term within its literary context.[24] Strangely, in an illustration toward the end of the book Irons inadvertently demonstrates the deficiency of his own project, namely, a focus and emphasis on lexical study over and against the theological function of a term in its immediate context! He writes:

> An exhaustive study of the word 'glasses' in the corpus of English literature would not help us in these cases. Such a study can only provide us with these possible meanings of the word, and perhaps a number of additional specialized uses and connotations. The context of English literature will only enable us to establish the semantic range available to a speaker or writer, but it will not enable us to determine which segment of that semantic range is being activated in any given instance.[25]

## A Critique of Irons' View of Judaism and the New Perspective

At various points throughout the monograph Irons' argues that the works of Hermann Cremer are foundational for the New Perspective, and he even suggests that the New Perspective understanding of the function of the word 'righteous' is "dependent" upon Cremer's theory.[26] What Irons is particularly concerned to accomplish in his book is to call into question the view of the New Perspective through a lexical study of the word *dikaiosunē* ("righteousness"). The New Perspective, built on the work of E.P.

22. Ibid., 126; cf. 146.

23. Ibid., 156; cf. 169; 178; 193; 195; 205; 207.

24. Ibid., 310 where Irons levels this charge against the adherents of the New Perspective who argue that "the righteousness of God" is a reference to the covenant faithfulness of God rather than a reference to the status declared to a believer. Of course, the New Perspective, in all of its various iterations, holds that the believers' status of righteousness is also very much present in the writings of Paul. In Romans and Galatians it is expressed through the verb *dikiaoō* which is typically declared 'to justify' and through the verb *logizomai* paired with a definite object from the *dik-* word group ("to reckon, declare, or count [righteous]"). In Phil 3, the concept of the human status of righteousness through faith is accomplished through the use of the Greek propositional phrase *ek Theou dikaiosunēn* ("the righteous status from God"). The New Perspective is merely arguing that in Romans and in Galatians the phrase *dikaiosunē Theou* ("the righteousness of God") is a reference to a characteristic of God, in those instances, and not to the status of human beings, which it nevertheless affirms through other grammatical constructions.

25. Ibid., 319.

26. Ibid., 156.

Sanders, critiqued Luther's view of Judaism in which the religion functioned as a foil to Christianity. In Luther's view, the problem with Judaism was that it was a meritorious, man-centered religion focused on the performance of "works-righteousness" which were undertaken by human beings in order to earn God's favor. Judaism, as the foil to Christianity, provides the negative backdrop for the pure Gospel of grace which is received through faith alone. The work of Sanders and others in the New Perspective movement have shown over the last 40 years or so that this caricature of Judaism as the epitome of "religion" in the negative sense was way off. Instead, Judaism was a religion of grace in which particularly Jewish works functioned, not as a means of earning one's salvation, but as covenant badges that showed that one belonged to the covenant community by God's gracious election. Thus, for the New Perspective, Christianity is not the solution to the foil of Judaism but it is rather *the fulfillment* of the covenant promises to Abraham that through him all the families of the earth would be blessed. This universally-aimed covenant, given before the Mosaic Law with its Jewish works of the Law, was brought about through the faithfulness of Jesus Christ for all who have faith, both the Jew and the Gentile alike. Following this line of thought, New Perspective proponents have argued generally that Luther's precise understanding of the Law and its relation to Christianity, as well as his understanding of "righteousness" have needed some major tweaking. These tweaks have included a revised and more historically nuanced and accurate view of Judaism as a religion of grace, and a more careful formulation of the doctrine of justification on the basis of the New Perspective's revised understanding and function of Jewish Law.

However, when one considers that these are the dynamics at play in scholarly discussion of the New Perspective's view of justification, it is shocking to me that there is not a single discussion about the phrase *erga tou nomou* ("works of the law") in this monograph. If, as Irons has expressly stated, the intent is to undermine the New Perspective, then surely this would require at least a brief treatment of the New Perspective's revised understanding of the nature and function of Jewish works of the law. Instead, Irons articulates the view of the New Perspective on page 3 of the monograph, and then does not address the issue until page 324 at which point he simply assumes the Old Perspective, Lutheran understanding of 'works' as (to use Irons favorite term) a cipher for religious "works-righteousness." Besides his lexical work on the term 'righteousness,' which, as we have observed, actually affirms the New Perspective view, Irons offers no substantial critique of the New Perspective. He shifts without justification (pun intended) into a position of presumption, simply restating, instead of arguing for, the old Lutheran view. For example, Irons states:

> There is, of course, a major difference between the understanding of this status in these Jewish writings and in Paul's theology: whereas for these Jewish writers, this status of righteousness before God is grounded in one's inherent righteousness that comes from obeying the law (what Paul would refer to as 'the righteousness of the law'), for Paul it comes from God as a gift of grace

received by faith on the ground of Christ's atoning death and resurrection (i.e., 'the righteousness of faith').[27]

Relatedly, while most would consider the language and idea of Judaism functioning as a 'foil' for Christianity to be a gross caricature, even of the Old Perspective, in a bizarre turn of events Irons actually adopts the phrase as a positive representation of his own view of Judaism! Whatever the theological understanding (or, I would say, misunderstanding) driving this view of Judaism, it is clear that Irons sees this pattern of religion in a variety of the canonical and extra canonical sources. For example, he argues that in 4 Maccabees it "may well be that the Jewish doctrine of the righteousness that comes from the Law that is the foil of the Pauline teaching finds its most articulate and sustained expression in 4 Maccabees."[28] He argues elsewhere that Paul has a polemic against "the nomistic theology of Judaism" and that this polemic can even be described as "anti-nomistic" (i.e. against-Law).[29]

## Conclusion

In conclusion I have leveled some heavy and sustained critique of Charles Lee Irons' monograph, *The Righteousness of God*. My intention is not to be overly severe but to be scholarly and bold. The preceding article is not meant to attack the hard work done by Dr. Irons, but merely to critically engage as a peer and fellow scholar of Paul, but to do so in an unabashedly forthright manner. To summarize my assessment of the book, I found the book to be a robust, scholarly lexical study of the term "righteousness" in antiquity. The level of detail and attention paid to the primary sources is exemplary. That being said, I took issue with three sets of elements in the book, namely: the methodology, the view of "righteousness" proposed by the author, and the view of Judaism assumed by the author. In regards to the methodology, I critiqued the approach that favored lexicography to the unnecessary and imprudent exclusion of a consideration of the theological function of a word in its particular contexts. Concerning Irons' view of "righteousness," I took issue with his view which emphasized only one aspect of "righteousness," namely, the forensic aspect, to the exclusion of the covenantal context in which forensic themes necessarily function in the canon of Holy Scripture. I also critiqued Irons' self-admission that although the word *dikaiosunē* does not mean "covenant faithfulness," the word can be shown

---

27. Ibid., 231-232. Emphasis mine.

28. Ibid., 239; cf. 314 where Irons argues that the ordinary understanding of Jewish works before Christianity is "a foil"; cf. the same 'foil' statement again on p. 339.

29. Ibid., 317. It should be noted that on p. 224 Irons does give a nod to E.P. Sanders, the pioneer of the New Perspective on Judaism that launched the New Perspective on Paul. He doesn't outright dismiss Sanders, but ultimately he does not support Sanders' view of covenantal nomism and instead defaults to the Old Perspective understanding of Judaism as a cipher of man-centered 'works-righteousness' religion.

to function in reference to the keeping of covenants and contracts. This attestation of usage in regard to covenant faithfulness, I argued, actually undermined his own argument rather than assisting in his attempt to undermine the New Perspective on Paul. Lastly, I drew attention to Irons' unsubstantiated adoption and articulation of perspectives on Judaism that I argued were not sufficiently established via scholarly argument in the monograph. The result was an infusion of Old Perspective theological presuppositions which were read into the various texts resulting in flawed exegetical results.

# *Response to Two Reviews of The Righteousness Of God*

## Charles Lee Irons

Charles Lee Irons has a Ph.D. in New Testament from Fuller Theological Seminary and serves as an Adjunct Professor at the California Graduate School of Theology

### Introduction

This dialogue presents an opportunity to review some of the significant differences between the New Perspective on Paul (NPP) and what some have called the Old Perspective on Paul. The NPP rests on three pillars. The first pillar is the new view of Judaism championed by E. P. Sanders in his well-argued and massively documented book, *Paul and Palestinian Judaism*.[1] Sanders showed that Pauline scholars were working with a caricature of the religion of Judaism in Paul's day. Rather than being a religion devoid of grace, it conformed to a pattern Sanders dubbed "covenantal nomism." This means that the grace of God is the prior basis on which he gave the law, and that the Jews are obligated to keep the law, not in order to earn God's favor, but to remain within the covenant. Only those who apostatized by rejecting the covenant (the Torah) were excluded. Those who repented of their sins, sought forgiveness, and attempted to live faithfully in accordance with the Torah would be saved eschatologically.

The second pillar of the NPP follows from the first. If Judaism is no longer understood as a religion of seeking to earn God's favor by works-righteousness, then what was Paul arguing against when he said that humans are justified not by "the works of the law" (*erga nomou*)[2] but by the faith of Jesus Christ? It sounds as if he is polemicizing against a view that does make justification by works. New Perspective scholars, most notably James D. G. Dunn and N. T. Wright, resolve the dilemma by reinterpreting the phrase. According to them, "the works of the law" are not the good moral deeds required by the law, but Israel's ethnocentric pride, supposed favored-nation status, and the boundary markers that set the Jews apart from the Gentiles. Paul is not contrasting works versus faith as the means of righteousness but racial sectarianism versus identification with Christ by the badge of faith. The gospel is that God's grace

---

1. E. P. Sanders, *Paul and Palestinian Judaism: A Comparison of Patterns of Religion* (Minneapolis: Fortress Press, 1977).
2. Paul uses the phrase "the works of the law" in Rom 3:20, 28; Gal 2:16; 3:2, 5, 10.

is not exclusive to the Jews, since God welcomes into his family anyone who has faith in Jesus, whether Jew or Gentile.

The first two pillars of the NPP have received excellent critiques from Old Perspective scholars, but there is a third pillar that has received less sustained attention, and that is the notion that Paul's "righteousness" and "justification" language is to be understood covenantally. Specifically, it is claimed, the noun "righteousness" can mean "covenant faithfulness" or "covenant membership," and the verb "justify" can mean "reckon someone to be a member of the covenant." Of particular interest is the Pauline phrase, "the righteousness of God," which occurs in some form 10 times in his writings.[3] New Perspective scholars claim that "the righteousness of God" should be translated "God's covenant faithfulness." Both Dunn and Wright make that claim. It is at root a lexical claim, since they argue that the concept of God's righteousness must be understood in terms of its Hebraic meaning in the Old Testament and in Jewish literature, where, they argue, it has a technical meaning that sets it apart from the ordinary judicial and ethical meanings of righteousness in extra-biblical Greek. I have sought to subject the NPP claim that "the righteousness of God" in Paul denotes "God's covenant faithfulness" to critical examination and to argue for an Old Perspective interpretation, namely, that it means "a righteousness that comes from God." I argue that "the righteousness of God" is not God's own righteousness, viewed either as an attribute or an activity, but the legal standing of righteousness that all who believe in Jesus the Messiah receive from God as a gift.

I attempt to do this in my published dissertation, *The Righteousness of God: A Lexical Examination of the Covenant-Faithfulness Interpretation*.[4] I am honored that my monograph has received such thoughtful reviews for the inaugural issue of this journal. I appreciate the positive statements that both reviewers have made. Greever's comments are more favorable. Greever says he is in "fundamental agreement" with my thesis and believes I have "demonstrated convincingly and definitively that God's righteousness is not to be defined as or equated with God's covenant faithfulness." Although Frederick aligns himself more with the New Perspective, he recognizes the importance and value of my research. Frederick says that "in terms of exhaustive lexical comparative work, the monograph is exemplary" and is "a useful scholarly resource." He also thinks I have made a "solid and convincing case against Hermann Cremer's view" that righteousness is a thoroughly positive, relational concept in the

---

3. Some variant of the phrase is found in Rom 1:17; 3:5, 21-22, 25-26; 10:3 [2x]; 2 Cor 5:21; Phil 3:9. I contend that in Rom 3:5, 25-26 it denotes God's distributive justice, and in the other seven cases it means "the gift of (imputed) righteousness from God." The genitive modifier "of God" (or "his") can be taken as a genitive of possession or as a genitive of source, depending on the context.

4. Charles Lee Irons, *The Righteousness of God: A Lexical Examination of the Covenant-Faithfulness Interpretation*, Wissenschaftliche Untersuchungen zum Neuen Testament II/386 (Tübingen: Mohr Siebeck, 2015).

Bible.[5] These assessments are personally satisfying, since it means I was successful in my critique of Cremer's relational theory of righteousness. There may be much more to discuss and debate with regard to the broader theological issues surrounding the New Perspective, but I am pleased that my achievement with regard to the Cremer Hebraic/relational theory is recognized. Cremer's relational theory of righteousness has been hugely influential in 20th century scholarship to the point of being an unquestioned consensus enshrined in practically all theological dictionaries and word books. It is a reigning paradigm of biblical scholarship, both OT and NT, and is in turn the theoretical lexical basis of the NPP view that "the righteousness of God" in Paul means, denotes, and should be translated as "God's covenant faithfulness." Thus, the recognition that I have made a convincing case against the theory is noteworthy in itself, apart from the polemics over the NPP.

There is much that could be said by way of response to these two reviews, but I am going to focus on five areas of engagement raised by Frederick. One of these (the fourth) is also a concern raised by Greever, so I will respond to both together under that heading.

## 1. Theological Presuppositions

The first area of engagement has to do with exegetical method. Frederick charges that I conducted my exegesis with an unwarranted theological bias, particularly the bias of Reformed theology. As Frederick acknowledges, there is no such thing as presupposition-less exegesis, so he is not claiming that theological presuppositions are always bad. Yet he thinks in this case I approached exegesis "from an overly dogmatic perspective."

It should be noted that all of the passages he objects to are from Chapter 6 of my book, the chapter devoted to exegesis of "the righteousness of God" in Paul, and not from the preceding chapters devoted to the lexical analysis of "righteousness." In a section[6] devoted to analyzing the "of God" part of the Pauline phrase, I argued that it is a genitive of source, so that the phrase could be translated "a righteousness *from* God." I argued that taking "of God" as a genitive of source is consistent with a broader theological thread running through Paul's thought, namely, his frequent contrast between divine agency (which Paul calls God's "grace") and human agency. Paul operates with the assumption that anything in us that is spiritually good is "of God" and not "of ourselves" (e.g., 2 Cor 3:5; 4:7; cp. Eph 2:8-9; Phil 1:28). I cited several New Testament

---

5. Hermann Cremer, *Die paulinische Rechtfertigungslehre im Zusammenhange ihrer geschichtlichen Voraussetzungen* (Gütersloh: Bertelsmann, 1900). The title may be translated, *The Pauline Doctrine of Justification in the Context of Its Historical Presuppositions*. The historical presuppositions Cremer had in mind were primarily the salvific usage of God's "righteousness" (*tsedeq* and *tsedaqah*) in the Hebrew OT, particularly in the Psalms and Isaiah.

6. Irons, *The Righteousness of God*, 316-18.

scholars in support this reading of "the Pauline doctrine of grace."[7] I did not appeal to my theological presuppositions as evidence for the genitive of source interpretation, but to specific Pauline texts and scholarly commentary on those texts.[8]

I find it ironic that Frederick earlier faulted me for my failure to sufficiently examine broader theological themes. I am unclear why examining broader theological themes is a good thing in the cases where I allegedly failed to do it, but a bad thing in the cases where I actually did it. It would appear that appeals to broader theological themes are only good when they support the NPP. I admit that my exegesis of Paul was conducted from a broader view of Pauline theology. But I remain unconvinced that it led to distorted exegetical results. No doubt Frederick thinks it did, but he did not offer any evidence of that.

The real issue is whether my theological perspective casts doubt on the results of my lexical analysis of the word "righteousness" in the OT and Jewish literature. Is the phrase, "the righteousness of God" in the OT, in Jewish literature, or in Paul, a technical term for "God's covenant faithfulness"? This is not really a theological debate, because everyone acknowledges that Paul thinks God is faithful to his covenant promises. The question is: What does the phrase mean? The question can only be decided by lexical analysis.

## 2. Lexical Method

It is to the topic of lexical analysis that we now turn—the second area of engagement. Frederick finds fault with "the primacy of place [my lexical approach] gives to the meaning of words above . . . the determination of the theological function of a phrase in its theological context." He says that "too much autonomy" is given to words apart from their theological functions. My lexical method "seems to operate in a Platonic manner in which a generic meaning . . . governs and restricts how the word is allowed to operate in any given theological context."

But I do not understand how we can do exegesis in any other way. Lexical meaning *must* "govern and restrict" how words can be used theologically. Whatever further theological functions we think a word may have, they usually remain within a word's semantic range and do not arbitrarily break outside of that range to a whole other meaning in a completely different semantic field. If that does occur, it has to be

---

7. "The Pauline doctrine of grace" is not a code-word for Reformed or Calvinistic theology (that would be the plural, "the doctrines of grace"), but is a common phrase used in German NT scholarship, *die paulinische Gnadenlehre*.

8. The scholars I appealed to were Adolf Schlatter and Francis Watson, as well as the multi-author volume *Divine and Human Agency in Paul and His Cultural Environment*, edited by John M. G. Barclay and Simon J. Gathercole (London: T&T Clark, 2008). To the extent that these scholars' interpretations of Paul comport with a broadly Augustinian conception of grace, perhaps it is not so much because they are reading Paul with Augustinian blinders, as it is because Augustine himself was a good reader of Paul.

demonstrated with a high standard of proof. Of course, I believe words can have a variety of metaphorical extensions and contextual modulations, but these are normally "tethered" in some way to what the words actually mean lexically, that is, their lexical sense.

I am unsure how to read Frederick here. Does he really believe a word's "theological functions" can be totally unrelated and untethered to its lexical meaning? He seems to imply that when he writes that lexical study is "utterly useless" unless considered in tandem with theological function of a word. If that is what he means, we have a sharp disagreement on a fundamental principle of exegetical method. On this approach, we should give up trying to do responsible exegesis to determine Paul's intended meaning and just read his letters as we please, divining whatever "theological functions" we happen to think we see in the text. Exegesis then becomes a Rorschach inkblot exercise in which each exegete projects their own views onto the text.

But I doubt Frederick countenances that, so perhaps a more charitable reading is possible. Let's set aside his unfortunate use of the phrase "utterly useless." Perhaps what he is trying to say is that the theological function of a word in a particular theological context can be a further specification, extension, or application of its lexical sense. Rather than being "utterly useless," careful lexical study is necessary to establish the semantic range of the word. However, our work is not yet done, for we would still need to investigate further to see if there are any further specifications of meaning *within* that semantic range, that is, further "theological functions" arising from the use of the word in specific contexts. If that is all Frederick meant to say, then we are in agreement. In fact, that is precisely the approach I took in my investigation. First, I established the semantic range of "righteousness" in extra-biblical Greek (ch.3), in the Old Testament (ch.4), and in Jewish literature (ch.5). Having established the semantic range, I then turned in the chapter on Paul (ch.6) to ask whether there was any evidence of a particular theological function of the phrase "the righteousness of God" in Paul's writings in which the phrase was used to refer ("within the actual context of the discourse in which it is being used") to a broader theological concept such as God's covenant faithfulness. On this more charitable reading of Frederick, far from undermining my entire project, my word-study method is precisely the method called for.

More importantly, my word-study approach was necessary since the claim of Dunn, Wright, and others, going back at least to Käsemann, is that "the righteousness of God" in early Jewish literature is a technical term picked up by Paul. Wright says, "There is thus, I contend, an excellent case to be made out for reading the phrase as a clear Pauline *technical term* meaning 'the covenant-faithfulness of [Israel's] God.'"[9] And Paul picked up this technical meaning from the OT and the Jewish literature based upon the OT:

---

9. Wright, "On Becoming the Righteousness of God: 2 Corinthians 5:21," in *Pauline Theology. Vol. II: 1 & 2 Corinthians*, ed. David M. Hay (Minneapolis: Fortress Press, 1993), 200-208; see p. 203; emphasis added; brackets original.

When we meet a word or term which is used in a consistent way across a range of literature of a particular period, and when we then meet the same word or term in an author we are studying, the natural presumption is that the word or term means there what it meant elsewhere ... Careful exegesis of "God's righteousness," both in the Old Testament and in second-temple Judaism, indicates that, among the range of possible meanings, "faithfulness to the covenant" is high on the list.[10]

Since this claim is of a lexical nature, my examination of it had to be of a lexical nature. It is not simply a theological debate about some added theological functions of a word or phrase in Paul. It is a lexical semantic debate over the meaning of *dikaiosynē theou* primarily in OT/Jewish literature, and secondarily in Paul in conversation with Jewish thinking. Given the state of the question, I do not see how this debate can be resolved any other way than by conducting a careful study of the way the phrase is used in the OT and in Jewish literature. Frederick's finding fault with my word-study method leaves the impression that he is unfamiliar with the precise nature of the NPP claim.

## 3. Wright and Cremer

The third area of engagement is quite significant, for it has the potential to undercut a major plank in my argument. While I may have succeeded in critiquing Cremer, Frederick suggests, Wright's arguments are independent of Cremer and therefore they remain untouched and unscathed by my research. Frederick thinks my attempt to link Wright to Cremer is "a massive, improbable stretch." He adds, "A quick look through all of N. T. Wright's major works reveals that Cremer is never even mentioned!"

But as I showed in my book, a good case can be made that Wright is in fact reliant upon Cremer's Hebraic/relational theory of righteousness. This would be true even if Wright had never heard of Cremer. Scholarly ideas and paradigms are often conveyed to subsequent generations of scholars through intermediary scholarship that is itself dependent on the original source. The fact that Wright never cites Cremer directly means little in view of the evidence for his dependence on Cremer. Let's look at the evidence.

First, I would argue that Wright was influenced by Cremer indirectly, through the work of Ernst Käsemann.[11] In his commentary on Romans, commenting on "the righteousness of God" in Rom 1:17, Käsemann wrote:

> At least in the course of the last century we have freed ourselves from the Greek understanding of *dikaiosynē* as a norm of what is right for God and man

---

10. Wright, *Justification: God's Plan and Paul's Vision* (Downers Grove: IVP Academic, 2009), 49, 99.

11. Irons, *The Righteousness of God*, 7, 10, 37 n.121, 42, 46-47.

> ... Further progress is made with the insight (already Cremer, *Rechtfertigungslehre* ... ) that in biblical usage righteousness, which is essentially forensic, denotes a relation in which one is set ... To the extent that this interpretation is oriented to the OT motif of covenant faithfulness, it can plausibly explain why *dikaiosynē* never means penal righteousness in Paul.[12]

Even though Käsemann attempted to scrub covenantal thought from Paul, he nevertheless viewed "God's righteousness" in Rom 3:25-26 as a pre-Pauline Jewish-Christian technical term that had "original reference to God's covenant faithfulness."[13] Whether or not Wright was aware of Käsemann's dependence on Cremer, Käsemann himself was aware of it, since Cremer's *Die paulinische Rechtfertigungslehre* is cited three times by Käsemann in his discussion of "the righteousness of God" in Rom 1:17.[14]

Wright himself seems to have gotten the covenant-faithfulness interpretation from Käsemann. He acknowledges that Käsemann "is well aware that a natural meaning of the phrase [*dikaiosynē theou*] in early Christianity would include God's covenant faithfulness," adding that this meaning is "uppermost in the many instances cited by Käsemann and others in the [Jewish] background literature."[15] Where Wright disagrees with Käsemann is in the latter's theory that Paul deliberately amended the meaning of the phrase to make it a universal, cosmic term denoting God's eschatological saving power by which he reclaims all creation.[16] Wright takes issue with Käsemann's assumption that the covenant is narrow and nationalistic, and argues, rightly, that the Abrahamic covenant had in view the ultimate inclusion of the Gentiles and the cosmic renewal of all creation. What Käsemann separated, Wright keeps together: "The divine faithfulness to the covenant is the appointed means of the divine faithfulness to the creation."[17] Thus, while scrupling over one element of Käsemann's view, Wright can nonetheless say that Käsemann's understanding of the righteousness of God is "foundational" and "helped to create the context" for the NPP.[18]

---

12. Käsemann, *Commentary on Romans*, trans. and ed. Geoffrey W. Bromiley (Grand Rapids: Eerdmans, 1980), 24-25; referenced in Irons, *The Righteousness of God*, 42 n.145.

13. Käsemann, *Commentary on Romans*, 30.

14. Ibid., 21, 24, 25.

15. Wright, "A New Tübingen School? Ernst Käsemann and His Commentary on Romans," *Themelios* 7.3 (1982), 6-16; see p. 14. More recently, Wright has argued strongly that Käsemann never lost sight of the "covenant faithfulness" interpretation and in fact emphasized it more in his later lectures. Wright, "A New Perspective on Käsemann? Apocalyptic, Covenant, and the Righteousness of God," in *Studies in the Pauline Epistles: Essays in Honor of Douglas J. Moo*, ed. Matthew S. Harmon and Jay E. Smith (Grand Rapids: Zondervan, 2014), 243-58.

16. Wright, "A New Tübingen School?" Cp. his recent statements to the same effect in Wright, *Paul and His Recent Interpreters* (Minneapolis: Fortress Press, 2015), 19 n.29, 123, 148, 190.

17. Wright, *Paul and the Faithfulness of God* (Minneapolis: Fortress Press, 2013), 841.

18. Wright, *Paul and His Recent Interpreters*, 56.

Second, Wright quotes from the article on "Righteousness, Righteousness of God" by K. L. Onesti and M. T. Brauch in the *Dictionary of Paul and His Letters*.[19] Here is Wright's exact quote from that article, which he uses as an appeal to authority in support of his covenant-faithfulness interpretation:

> The concept of righteousness in the Hebrew Bible emphasizes the relational aspect of God and humanity in the context of a covenant . . . The Hebrew meaning of justice means more than the classical Greek idea of giving to every one their due. Usually the word suggests Yahweh's saving acts as evidence of God's faithfulness to the covenant. For this meaning of righteousness of God, *dikaiosynē* is not as flexible as the Hebrew word . . . An essential component of Israel's religious experience was that Yahweh was not only Lord of Law but also the one who was faithful to it. God was faithful to the covenant. God's righteousness was shown by saving actions in accordance with his covenant relationship . . . Righteousness is not primarily an ethical quality; rather it characterizes the character or action of God who deals rightly within a covenant relationship . . . The covenant faithfulness of God, the righteousness of God, is shown by Yahweh's saving acts.[20]

These are the words of Onesti and Brauch as quoted by Wright. A few pages later, Onesti and Brauch credit the originator of the covenant-faithfulness interpretation: "H. Cremer (1900) launched scholarship in a new direction by pointing to the OT understanding of *s<sup>e</sup>daqa* ('righteousness') as covenant faithfulness."[21] Cremer's paradigm shift was recognized by Brauch himself in an earlier essay on the same topic:

> A new turning point [from Luther's emphasis on the gift-character of righteousness] . . . was provided by H. Cremer in that he pointed to the Old Testament as the historical presupposition for Paul's conception of 'God's righteousness.' Cremer demonstrated that *dikaiosynē theou* must be understood in terms of *tsedaqah*, a 'relational concept' which designates the action of partners in keeping with the covenant (i.e., covenant-faithfulness).[22]

Thus, we have two pieces of evidence for Wright's dependence on Cremer: his own admission of reliance on Käsemann, who cited Cremer, and his appeal to the

---

19. K. L. Onesti and M. T. Brauch, "Righteousness, Righteousness of God," in *Dictionary of Paul and His Letters* (= *DPL*), ed. Gerald F. Hawthorne and Ralph P. Martin (Downers Grove: InterVarsity Press, 1993), 827-37. I noted Wright's reliance on this article in *The Righteousness of God*, 6 n20.

20. Wright, *Paul and the Faithfulness of God*, 800, quoting sentences from Onesti and Brauch, *DPL*, 828-29.

21. Onesti and Brauch, *DPL*, 834.

22. Manfred T. Brauch, "Perspectives on 'God's Righteousness' in recent German discussion," Appendix to Sanders, *Paul and Palestinian Judaism*, 525. This essay seems to have provided much of the basis for the later *DPL* article which was co-authored with Karen L. Onesti, then a Ph.D. candidate at the same institution with Brauch.

article by Onesti and Brauch, who explicitly acknowledged Cremer as a key "turning point" in the interpretation of the Pauline concept of "the righteousness of God."

Frederick gives the impression that in his magnum opus, *Paul and the Faithfulness of God*, Wright advances an independent, detailed lexical case for taking God's righteousness as his covenant faithfulness. But if one peruses the section of the book devoted to this topic, it becomes evident that such a detailed lexical case is lacking.[23] Wright quotes some verses from the OT where the righteousness of God is used in significant theological contexts (especially Isaiah 40-55), but he quotes them without making any arguments. He just asserts that God's righteousness in these texts means God's covenant faithfulness. Even more glaring is the omission of any discussion of "the righteousness of God" in the Jewish literature (the Dead Sea Scrolls, the OT Apocrypha, the OT Pseudepigrapha, Hellenistic Jewish literature, Philo, and Josephus). Wright does not provide original scholarly arguments of a lexical nature defending his view and instead relies on the prior scholarship of Käsemann, Onesti, and Brauch, who were in turn explicitly relying on Cremer.

## 4. Righteousness and Covenant

We come now to the fourth area of engagement, the one where both reviewers registered similar concerns. Both Greever and Frederick take issue with my separation of righteousness from covenant. Greever thinks I merely overstated the distinction between righteousness and covenant, whereas Frederick thinks I made a major exegetical error in advocating a non-covenantal definition of righteousness.

The first thing to say by way of response is that I do not wish to be understood as saying that Paul's doctrine of justification is a non-covenantal concept. I stated that one of my goals was "to rescue the interpretation of Paul's doctrine of justification from *inappropriate* covenantal categories."[24] I did not say that I was seeking to rescue Paul's doctrine of justification from all covenantal categories, but only from inappropriate ones. The inappropriate covenantal categories that I had in mind were those provided by the Cremer theory that "righteousness" in Paul has a Hebraic technical meaning having to do with "covenant faithfulness" or "covenant membership." I am opposing this particular covenantal interpretation of Paul's justification and righteousness language, not all covenantal interpretations. Indeed, covenant theology plays an architectonic role in my own understanding of biblical theology in general and of the Pauline doctrine of justification in particular.

Furthermore, I agree that "righteousness" in biblical theology has a definite covenantal context. That is to say, the biblical theological concept of "righteousness" cannot

---

23. Wright, *Paul and the Faithfulness of God*, 795-804. In the Subject Index, the entry for "Righteousness, of God" lists this 10-page section first. In *Paul and His Recent Interpreters* (e.g., p. 148 n.6), Wright again refers readers to this section.

24. Irons, *The Righteousness of God*, 6; emphasis added.

be rightly understood without reference to a specific biblical covenant. We bring the concept of covenant into the discussion of "righteousness" in biblical theology as soon as we inquire about the standard of judgment. In my book, I did just that.[25] I argued, against Cremer, that righteousness is not a relational concept in which the relationship itself is the norm, so that if one is faithful to the relationship or covenant, then one is righteous. In opposition to Cremer, I argued for the traditional pre-Cremer view that "righteousness" is a norm concept. But of course this raises the question, "What is the norm of righteousness in the Bible?" It is here that the covenant enters in. If the question is the judgment of the nations, then I would argue that natural law is the standard—and I take natural law to be covenantal, since it is rooted in the pre-Fall Adamic covenant of works. If the question is the judgment of God's covenant people, then the Mosaic Law (the Sinai covenant) is the standard of judgment defining what is righteous and what is unrighteous. So it is not true that I have created a complete separation between righteousness and covenant.

However, I maintain that "righteousness" is not a covenantal word. It may sound as though I have just contradicted myself, but hear me out. This paradox is characteristic of many words in the biblical lexicon. Take the word "redemption" and its cognates such as "redeem," "ransom," etc. The word-group is profiled against the base of the human experience, common in the ancient world, of buying back something or someone by paying the redemption price.[26] Slaves could be redeemed by paying a redemption price. Property (physical land) that had been transferred from one family to another could be redeemed or bought back. The concept of "redemption" is not profiled against the base of covenant. To understand the conceptual metaphor of redemption you don't analyze the social world of the $b^e rith$—covenant ratification rituals, oaths, treaties, promises, stipulations, blessings and curses, and so on. Redemption has nothing to do with covenant. That may sound like overstatement, but it is literally true. Redemption, either as a word or as a concept, is not an inherently covenantal activity. It doesn't live and move and have its being within the conceptual frame of covenant. It is a fundamentally commercial concept having to do with buying back things (land) or people (slaves) that had become alienated from their original owners by paying the required price so as to re-acquire ownership of them.

Nevertheless, when we move from the field of lexicography to the field of biblical theology, the biblical-theological concept of "redemption" must be understood in light of the larger covenantal context. God "redeemed" Israel from the house of bondage in Egypt because he was keeping the promises he made in the Abrahamic covenant (Exod 2:23-24; 3:6; 4:5; 6:2-8; Deut 7:8). In the new covenant, the blood of

---

25. Ibid., 162-63.

26. Base-profile analysis comes from one of the founders of cognitive linguistics, Ronald W. Langacker. He gives the example of *hypotenuse*, a concept that only makes sense in terms of its setting within the geometric interrelationships of a right triangle. Thus, the term *hypotenuse* is "profiled" against the "base" of the right triangle. See Irons, *The Righteousness of God*, 120 n.25, 126.

Christ is the payment price, and his blood is the blood of the covenant (Matt 20:28; 26:28). Salvation is construed through the lens of a conceptual metaphor taken from the commercial realm of redeeming slaves from slavery by paying the ransom price. But because God's act of saving and forming his people is covenantal, when the redemption metaphor is utilized to conceptualize salvation, the biblical-theological concept of redemption is also covenantal.[27]

When writing an article on the biblical theology of "redemption," a biblical theologian would need to explain the covenantal context of "redemption." But when writing an entry for a lexicon, a lexicographer is more narrowly focused on the lexical meaning of the word, which must be derived from careful analysis of the word's relation to other members of its semantic domain, its semantic range, its base-profile configuration, its underlying conceptual significance, and various metaphorical extensions of meaning. Possibly some of the notable contextual modulations of the lexical meaning may be mentioned in a lexicon, particularly a lexicon devoted to a particular corpus (such as the Hebrew OT, the Greek OT, or the Greek NT), but these contextual modulations would have to be carefully distinguished from the lexical meaning, since contextual modulations are usage-specific and any additional shades of meaning are derived from the context and are not part of the lexical value of the word itself. This was the point of the opening section of my chapter on methodology, where I carefully established the crucially important distinction between "lexical concepts" and "discourse concepts."[28] This was a key methodological presupposition that laid the groundwork for the rest of the argument as it unfolds in my book.

To return to "righteousness," I claim that "righteousness," is not strictly a covenantal word, even though in biblical theology it functions within a broader covenantal context. In other words, "righteousness" is not profiled against the base of "covenant." To understand what biblical "righteousness" words mean and how they operate lexically, you don't analyze the social world of b<sup>e</sup>rith-making. You analyze, in the first place, the social world of judicial activity in a court setting, and secondarily the realm of moral or ethical behavior, which is plausibly viewed as a metaphorical extension of the court setting. Once you have done that, of course, you can then move on to engage in a broader theological analysis, showing how this fundamentally judicial metaphor is employed covenantally in biblical theology.

---

27. All theology is highly metaphorical, that is, it uses realities of embodied experience from ordinary daily life to describe or construe spiritual realities. For a primer on conceptual metaphor, see George Lakoff and Mark Johnson, *Metaphors We Live By* (Chicago: The University of Chicago Press, 1980; reprinted with an Afterword, 2003).

28. Irons, *The Righteousness of God*, 61-65.

## 5. The Role of Works in Judaism

The final area of engagement has to do with the role of works in the Jewish religion of Paul's context. Frederick thinks my work relies on a pre-Sanders understanding of Judaism. He says he is shocked that I did not discuss the Pauline phrase *erga nomou* ("the works of the law").

In my defense, one can only do so much in a dissertation or any book for that matter. Doctoral supervisors typically counsel their students to make sure their dissertation topic is narrowly focused. Instead of engaging that exegetical debate, I chose to point the reader to the work of others who have, in my view, provided satisfactory responses on these other aspects of the NPP. I thought the issues of Sanders's "covenantal nomism" and "the works of the law" had been sufficiently addressed by a number of important studies.[29] In my dissertation, I wanted to focus on an aspect of the NPP that I felt had not yet been addressed in detail by the critics of the NPP. It would have made an already long book even longer if I had chosen to rehash the exegetical debate over "the works of the law."

Space forbids me to examine that exegetical debate here, but I do want to point out that Frederick mischaracterizes my view of Judaism. He presumes I hold that Judaism was a man-centered religion devoid of grace in which works-righteousness was performed with a view to earning God's favor. I never wrote that anywhere in my book, and the sentence he quotes doesn't say that.[30] The term "works-righteousness" is not one that I used. It is a loaded term, with connotations of a self-righteous legalism that has no need for the grace of God.

Let me take this opportunity to explain more explicitly what I think about the character of the religion of Judaism in Paul's day. To begin with, I think Sanders was right to issue a corrective against the view of many older New Testament scholars that early Judaism had no concept of God's grace, denied the possibility of repentance and forgiveness, and was bent on trying to earn or merit God's favor by works. Sanders provided overwhelming textual evidence from early Jewish literature demonstrating that the Jews did believe in the priority of God's grace, and not all Jews had a crass mentality of trying to earn eschatological life apart from God's grace. *Paul*

---

29. Andrew A. Das, *Paul, the Law, and the Covenant* (Peabody: Hendrickson, 2001); idem, "Beyond Covenantal Nomism: Paul, Judaism, and Perfect Obedience," *Concordia Journal* 27 (2001): 234-52; Simon J. Gathercole, *Where Is Boasting? Early Jewish Soteriology and Paul's Response in Romans 1-5* (Grand Rapids: Eerdmans, 2002); Seyoon Kim, *Paul and the New Perspective: Second Thoughts on the Origin of Paul's Gospel* (Grand Rapids: Eerdmans, 2002); Peter Stuhlmacher, *Revisiting Paul's Doctrine of Justification: A Challenge to the New Perspective*, with an essay by Donald A. Hagner (Downers Grove: InterVarsity, 2001); Charles H. Talbert, "Paul, Judaism, and the Revisionists," *CBQ* 63 (2001): 1-22; Stephen Westerholm, *Perspectives Old and New on Paul: The "Lutheran" Paul and His Critics* (Grand Rapids: Eerdmans, 2004); idem, "The Righteousness of the Law and the Righteousness of Faith in Romans," *Interpretation* 58 (July 2004): 253-64. I refer to these scholarly critiques of the NPP in *The Righteousness of God*, 5 n.16; 6 n.21.

30. "There is, of course, a major difference ..." (Irons, *The Righteousness of God*, 231-32).

*and Palestinian Judaism* is a masterful piece of scholarship that exploded widely-held scholarly assumptions.

However, I think Sanders himself swung the pendulum too far in the opposite direction when he failed to recognize the importance within Judaism of law-keeping as the means to attaining a status of righteousness before God. While God's grace was prior to the giving of the Torah (law) and forgiveness was available to those who repented of their sins, repentance only put one back on the path of trying to obey the law in order to be righteous.[31] Righteousness was not viewed as a gift freely given by God (as in Paul), but as God's recognition of a person's own righteousness which comes from personal obedience to the law. On this construction, it is not necessary to caricature Judaism as a "man-centered" religion of "works-righteousness." The Jews would have said, "It is not man-centered to obey God's law; God revealed it precisely so that we might obey it!" To make sense of Paul's teaching, however, it is necessary to maintain that many Jews typically thought they had to obey the law in order to be righteous before God.[32] This construction of Judaism's view of "the righteousness that comes from the law" seems to be presupposed in several key Pauline passages (e.g., Rom 3:20-28; 9:30–10:6; Gal 2:16; Phil 3:9). I realize that these passages are contested, but the scholars cited above have, in my view, brought needed balance to Sanders's overly sanguine view of Judaism and answered the NPP's interpretation of "the works of the law."

## The Importance of this Discussion

I have spent most of my space responding to Frederick's critical review, but in conclusion, I want to say that I agree with Greever's assessment of the importance of this subject: "The reason why this issue should be taken seriously is that it has everything to do with how an individual can be assured of final justification." Paul stated that he was not ashamed of the gospel because it is "the power of God for salvation," and it is that power because "in it the righteousness of God is revealed" (Rom 1:16-17). Thus, for Paul, the righteousness of God stands at the very heart of the gospel that he preached. I agree with NPP scholars, and with Wright in particular, that God is faithful to his covenant promises given to Abraham. I would even agree that that truth

---

31. As I explained in my discussion of Jewish soteriology in ibid., 223-25.

32. For example, here is a quote from the *Psalms of Solomon*, an early Jewish text written in the century before Paul: "Our works are in the choosing and power of our soul, to do righteousness or injustice in the works of our hands, and in your righteousness you visit human beings. The one who does righteousness stores up life for himself with the Lord, and the one who practices injustice is responsible for the destruction of his own soul, for the judgments of the Lord are in righteousness for each man and household" (*Ps. Sol.* 9:4-5). This same writing also recognizes God's mercy (*Pss. Sol.* 3:5-8; 9:6-8; 15:13), so clearly this is not a religion devoid of grace. Yet righteousness is not a gift from God but something that a person must "do" in order to "store up life" with the Lord and avoid destruction of their soul. See my discussion of the *Pss. Sol.* in *The Righteousness of God*, 222-25.

stands at the heart of the gospel (Rom 1:2; 4:16, 21; 15:8; 2 Cor 1:20; Gal 3:8, 18, 29). But as true as that is theologically, my claim is that when Paul uses the phrase "the righteousness of God" in Rom 1:17 (and in Rom 3:21-22; 10:3, 2 Cor 5:21; Phil 3:9), he is not giving expression to that theological truth, important as it may be, but is rather referring to the status of righteousness that comes from God as a gift. Paul says this was what Abraham found—the standing of being "righteous" or "justified" before God, a standing he had, not because he did the good works of obedience demanded by the law, but because he simply believed in God's promise (Rom 4). That is what makes the gospel the power of God for salvation—the fact that it reveals Jesus Christ, crucified and risen, as the one on whose account sinners may be accepted as righteous before God. This righteousness from God, not our own righteousness, is the basis of our confident assurance that at the last day when we stand before the judge of all the earth, we will not be condemned but will be inheritors, as Abraham's offspring, of eternal life in the new creation.

# BOOK REVIEWS

**Robertson, Palmer O.** *The Flow of the Psalms: Discovering Their Structure and Theology.* Phillipsburg, NJ: P&R, 2015, pp. 302, $ 21.99, paperback.

O. Palmer Robertson is director and principle of African Bible University in Uganda and is the author of many books, including *The Christ of the Covenants* (P&R, 1987), commentaries on the books of Nahum, Habakkuk, and Zephaniah in the *New International Commentary Series* (Eerdmans, 1990), and *The Christ of the Prophets* (P&R, 2008). His latest work, *The Flow of the Psalms: Discovering Their Structure and Theology*, represents one of the most recent contributions to the ongoing investigation of the "shape" and "shaping" of the Hebrew Psalter. Robertson's burden in this book is to show that the Psalter is not a random collection of psalms; rather, it exhibits an intentional arrangement or "flow" from beginning to end (p. 50).

Two preliminary chapters precede Robertson's attempt to demonstrate the presence of this "flow" within the Psalter. Chapter two draws attention to twelve different elements of basis structure in the Psalter, while chapter three is devoted to a discussion of the Psalter's redemptive-historical framework. The heart of the book then follows in chapters five through nine, where Robertson traces the predominant structural, theological, and thematic contours of each of the Psalter's five books. The major thematic focus of Book I (Pss 1–41) is said to be *confrontation*. This book predominantly reflects the constant confrontation between Israel's messianic king (i.e., David) and his enemies as he attempts to establish his messianic kingdom (p. 53). A prominent structural feature of this book is the strategic placement of four acrostic psalms (Pss 9/10, 25, 34, and 37) to divide this large book into smaller units and, thereby, to aid in its memorization (p. 81).

Book II (Pss 42–72) witnesses a progression from David's personal struggle to establish his kingship to the struggle between the people of Elohim and their corporate enemies (p. 90). But while struggle continues, the psalmist's effort to *communicate* a message of hope to his enemies arises as the distinctive message of Book II (p. 107). The thematic focus of Book III (Pss 73–89) is *devastation*. In these seventeen psalms, Robertson detects a shift in perspective to the corporate community of God's people and their devastation by international forces (p. 122).

The perspective of the Psalter shifts once again in Book IV (Pss 90–106). The distinctive focus of this book is that exile brought *maturation* to the people of God (pp. 147–148). The refrain "*Yahweh Malak*" ("Yahweh is King") emerges as a distinctive statement in this book, triumphantly declared in the midst of the distress of exile

(p. 153). At the same time, Book IV also encourages "a resurgence of hope in the kingdom of the Davidic Messiah" (p. 147). Finally, the *consummation* of the kingdom of God is the major theme of Book V (Pss 107–150) (p. 184). As with Book IV, Book V also fosters hope in a Davidic Messiah, as evidenced by the presence of fifteen Davidic psalms (Pss 108–110, 122, 124, 131, 133, and 138–145) (pp. 190–195, 224–229).

Robertson's work contributes to the ongoing discussion of the Psalter's canonical shape in at least the following three areas. First, it makes important methodological contributions. While, like other similar studies, he takes into consideration psalm titles, genre, and key-word associations, for Robertson the *substance* of the psalms "overrides all other considerations of structure" (p. 239; see also p. 52 n. 6 and p. 92 n. 8). Throughout the book he demonstrates how this focus has the potential to shed new light on the Psalter's structure. To give only one example, even though Pss 49–50 and 51–52 are attributed to different authors, Robertson contends that an analysis of their content uncovers a chiastic structure that binds these four psalms together (pp. 90–95). Focusing primarily on the psalm titles in this section of the Psalter, previous studies (e.g., Wilson's *Editing of the Hebrew Psalter*) have overlooked this possibility. A second methodological contribution is the way in which Robertson attempts to take *all* of the evidence into consideration in reaching conclusions about the Psalter's structure and message. For example, rather than concentrating only on psalms that most clearly support his thesis, Robertson attempts to show how *each* of the seventeen psalms in Book III supports his contention that the book's major theme is "devastation" (pp. 122–146). Such is a welcome corrective in an area of study where, all too often, claims about the Psalter's structure or message are based primarily upon a select group of psalms, such as those appearing at the opening or closing "seams" of the five books (e.g., Wilson's *The Editing of the Hebrew Psalter* [SBL, 1985]; deClaissé-Walford's *Reading from the Beginning* [Mercer, 1997]).

A further contribution is Robertson's concern to trace the pastoral implications of the Psalter's canonical shape. An illustration of this concern comes from his discussion of the structural role played by acrostic psalms in Book I. He observes that Pss 34 and 37 bracket four psalms of the innocent sufferer (Pss 34–37) and are followed by four psalms of the guilty sufferer (Pss 38–41). Robertson then points to the pastoral value of his structural observations: "a pastor who is aware of the bracketing function of acrostics 34 and 37 could be significantly helped in counseling persons struggling with either innocence of guilt in their response to suffering" (p. 80). Another example is found in the conclusion of this same section. Robertson discusses how attention to the structural role of the acrostics in Book I "could serve as a great blessing for the church of Jesus Christ today" by aiding in memorization of the majority of the book (p. 82).

A final contribution to be mentioned is the author's suggestion that the structure of the Psalter may have impacted the New Testament authors' usage of psalms. Robertson asks, for example, how John, Luke, and Paul could use the same psalm (i.e.,

Ps 69) to support four different aspects of redemptive history (p. 117). In response to this question, he suggests that "the position of this psalm immediately after the "dialogue" between the cry for help of the messianic king and the affirmation of God's undisturbed reign (Pss 61–68) could provide a partial answer" (p. 117). Similarly, he suggests that the quote from Ps 82:6 in John 10:34 may have been based upon the author's knowledge of the psalm's broader context. According to Robertson, this context is a deliberately arranged group of psalms (Pss 77–83) that centers on Ps 80, a psalm presenting Messiah as God's "Son" who suffers and is gloried (pp. 136–137).

This book will appeal to any serious student of the Psalter. Accessible enough for the novice, especially those looking for an entry point into the exciting study of the Psalter's canonical shape, Robertson's thought-provoking analysis and interaction with the scholarly literature makes this book both appealing and valuable to the specialist as well. *The Flow of the Psalms* is a welcome contribution to Psalms studies.

Stephen J. Smith
The Southern Baptist Theological Seminary, Louisville, KY

**Sanders, E. P. *Paul: The Apostle's Life, Letters, and Thought*. Minneapolis: Fortress, 2015, pp. 777, $39, paperback.**

E. P. Sanders is one of the most well-known New Testament scholars in the world today due to the tremendous influence of his 1977 book *Paul and Palestinian Judaism*. His commanding explanation of the "pattern of religion" found in rabbinic and Second Temple Jewish sources turned Pauline scholarship away from previous caricatures of Judaism to a fresh interaction with the primary sources. It also laid the foundation for the "new perspective" on Paul.

But although we are familiar with Sanders the scholar, in this book we meet Sanders the teacher. *Paul* is a book written by the retired Duke professor for undergraduate students. It is a complete exposition of the apostle's undisputed letters, and, while Sanders has written several books on Paul, this is the first one in which he addresses all of Paul's thought in one place. This book gives us another side of Sanders— here we get a peek inside of his lecture hall where Sanders quotes Shakespeare, Milton, Kipling, and Poe; explains how he teaches his Greek students to bring out the force of Paul's phrase *me genoito* ("Hell, no!"); tells us how striking he finds Paul's boasting in weakness and that Galatians 3:6–29 is his "favorite argument in the whole world" (p.536); notes his great admiration for the commentaries of J. B. Lightfoot; and even recounts the conclusions of previous student term papers.

The book begins with four chapters on Paul's life, examining the evidence of both Acts and Paul's letters. He tends to see contradictions between these two bodies of evidence rather than attempting to harmonize apparent discrepancies. He emphasizes Paul's background in the Greek-speaking Diaspora, questioning the claim of Acts that

Paul's education was in Jerusalem and arguing against Martin Hengel that "Hebrew of Hebrews" (Phil 3:5) does not refer to Paul's ability to speak Hebrew but rather to Paul's lineage (pp.24-28). Sanders argues that we do not see many traces of unique Pharisaic ideas like precise application of the law in Paul's letters (p.54) and that Paul's role in persecution was not linked particularly to his being a Pharisee (pp.80-81). In this section we see a glimpse into Sanders' great learning of ancient Jewish literature, but in my view he probably overemphasizes Paul's background in the Greek-speaking Diaspora. For example, Sanders suggests that Paul's Bible was the LXX (the Greek translation of the Hebrew Bible) which he had probably memorized as a boy (pp.60-62, 72-76). But while Paul certainly made use of these Greek translations and he may have memorized them, his quotations sometimes differ from our copies of the LXX and follow our copies of the Hebrew Bible (MT) instead. Further, Paul never claims the inspiration of the Greek translation as Philo does of the Greek translation of the law (*Life of Moses* II.37).

Was Paul converted to Christianity? Sanders rightly notes that this common question is really is a debate over the meaning of "conversion"—if it means that Paul "turned from" the Jewish God then he did not convert, but if it means that he "turned to" a new revelation of the Lord then we can say he was converted (2 Cor 3:16) (pp.101-102). Sanders argues that Paul then became apostle to the Gentiles and only indirectly to the Jews (appealing to Rom 11 and seeing a contradiction with Acts). In typical Sanders fashion, he summarizes the apostle's message under several bullet points: "(1) God had sent his Son; (2) he suffered and died by crucifixion for the benefit of humanity; (3) he was raised and was now in heaven; (4) he would soon return; and (5) those who belonged to him would live with him forever" (p.119). He then offers some interesting reflection on how Paul traveled (probably by foot) and how he financed his journeys (not by inherited wealth but through patrons). Some reflection on 1 Corinthians 9 might have rounded out the picture here.

The heart of this book comprises nineteen chapters on Paul's letters, in which Sanders the teacher engages their major "topics" (an important exercise in which he makes his students engage). Two chapters introduce the letters, followed by two on 1 Thessalonians, seven on the Corinthian correspondence, four on Galatians, one on Philippians, and three on Romans. Sanders only covers the seven letters whose authorship is undisputed (really six, as he does not discuss Philemon in depth). So he does not discuss Ephesians, Colossians, 2 Thessalonians, 1 Timothy, 2 Timothy, or Titus. I can't imagine how long this book would be if he discussed all thirteen! He argues that Paul dictated the letters himself, that he did not revise them, and that "they reveal his mind at work" (p.155). He very tentatively holds to John Knox's position that Onesimus the runaway slave later became the bishop of Ephesus and compiled Paul's letter collection (pp.155-57). Finally, he takes a chronological approach in his presentation because he has come to the conclusion that it is important to study *development* in Paul's thought (a change from his earlier view [p. xxxi]). By "development"

Sanders does not mean that Paul changed or retracted his earlier positions but that he grew in his understanding of the significance of Christ Jesus (p.172). At the end of the day Sanders most discusses development in Paul's eschatology as Paul wrestled with the imminence of the Lord's return.

Regarding matters of introduction, Sanders argues that 2 Corinthians has been edited. Originally 2 Corinthians 10-13 was the painful letter written before 2 Corinthians 1–9 (p.231). It is also possible that 2 Corinthians 6:14—7:1 is part of the letter that Paul wrote the church before 1 Corinthians (ibid.). While he sees merit in the idea that the difficult 1 Corinthians 14:33b-36 was a secondary edition, he ultimately argues that Paul is probably answering different questions, "one about head-coverings (chap. 11) and one about one particular female member on the congregation who tried to do all the talking (chap. 14)" (p.286) The two pieces of advice are truly contradictory—"the one *true contradiction* in Paul's letters of which I am aware" (p.287). But it is only a contradiction in that Paul applies one maxim in one case and another in another (ibid.). Sanders views 2 Corinthians 8–9 as the last part of the Corinthian correspondence (p.434). He holds to the North Galatian Theory of the audience of Galatians, and he suggests that the letter must have been written after Corinthians but before Romans because of theological developments (p.448). Philippians was written between Galatians and Romans during an imprisonment in Ephesus (pp.582-83). And Romans was Paul's final letter whose main theme is the equality of Jews and Gentiles before God (p.615).

One of major theses of this book is that students and scholars should distinguish Paul's conclusions and the reasons for those conclusions from Paul's actual arguments as they are presented in his letters. Paul's conclusions are usually clear, but his *arguments* are what make him so difficult to understand (p. xvi). Moreover, Paul's conclusions typically came to him before he had formulated his arguments (p. xxviii). Readers familiar with Sanders will recognize this statement as a variation of his well-known idea that for Paul the "solution" of Jesus Christ came to him before he developed the "plight" of human sinfulness. Finally, Sanders argues that we should assume that Paul's conclusions were more important to him than his arguments (ibid.). This line of thought comes up so frequently in the book that I do not think it is an overstatement to call it the most important idea of the book (e.g., pp.283, 315, 466, 473, 536-37, 628, 654). In my view, it is also one the weakest ideas of the book. While Sanders is probably correct to observe that Paul worked out his arguments after coming to his conclusions, does he expect us to believe that Paul did not actually think his arguments were important, valid, and true (i.e., good reasons to come to this conclusion)? Granted, we can sometimes overstate our arguments in the midst of a heated verbal debate. But was Paul constantly doing that in his written letters—making arguments he knew to be incorrect because he was so convinced of his conclusions? If we asked Paul, "Are your arguments good arguments?" would he say "no, I just said that because I was so convinced of my conclusion for other reasons." This view seems unlikely to me. With that said, I do think Sanders makes a helpful point that Paul's arguments are those of a first-century Jew, and this is why he is sometimes so confusing to modern readers (e.g., the typological argument of 1 Cor 10:6-13 [p.315]).

Some of the major theses of this book peak to the issues at the heart of the new perspective on Paul. Sanders argues throughout for a sharp separation between "works of the law" and good deeds in Paul's letters (p.498). "Works of the law" in Galatians and Romans refer mainly to circumcision (p.513; 630), not charitable deeds (p.562). This is a well-known position of the new perspective, and Sanders is sometimes very strong on this point: "These verses against reliance on 'works of the law' are often converted into reliance on 'good works or 'good deeds,' the sorts of things for which Boy Scouts and others are applauded. And then it is thought that Paul was against 'good deeds.' Nothing could be a worse perversion of what Paul wrote. As we have seen several times, he was 100 percent in favor of good deeds and urged people to do more and more (1 Thess. 4:10)" (p.630). Sanders is right that Paul says Christians should pursue good works and "fulfill" the law through love of neighbor. He is also right that circumcision is the major issue in Paul's statements about "works of the law" in Galatians. But he fails to interact with the many critics of the new perspective who point out that Paul's statements against relying on "works of the law" actually do refer to moral obedience and not merely the boundary markers that distinguished Jews from Gentiles—e.g., Paul's statement that no one will be justified by works of the law in Romans 3:20 concludes an argument which accuses all people of being under the power of sin or not having done what is good (cf. Rom 4:6-8 and Rom 9:11).

I was very interested to see that Sanders continues to emphasize a point often quoted from *Paul and Palestinian Judaism*—namely, the idea that Paul's most important criticism of Judaism is that it was not Christianity. Paul's most important critique was certainly not legalism (a point Sanders makes very clear), and it was not even a critique of ethnocentrism (as many other new perspective scholars have argued). Rather, "According to Rom. 10:1-4, *what is wrong with the Jews is that they are not Christian; what is wrong with Judaism is that it does not accept Christianity*" (681; cf. 536-37, pp.610-611, and 611n35). There is certainly truth in this claim. At the heart of Paul's critique of Judaism is that the Jewish people as a whole did not confess Jesus as Lord. However, Paul's logic in Romans 9:30-33 and 10:1-4, two parallel passages that basically make the same point, is that it was their attempt to establish their own righteousness with the law that actually led the Jewish people away from believing in Christ (on this important criticism of the new perspective see Dane Ortlund's *Zeal Without Knowledge*, Bloomsbury, 2014). In other words, Paul does seem to have a category for a kind of "self-righteousness" that leads one away from accepting the righteousness of God through faith in Christ. How does Sanders respond to this logic? Romans 9:30-33 represents Paul's argument, not his actual conclusion (pp.677-80).

As a critic of the new perspective, I clearly disagree with some of Sanders's conclusions. But even on these contested issues of Paul and the Law, I think his observations are helpful—e.g., the way he frames Paul's wrestling with "two dispensations" (the coming of the law and the coming of Christ). He really listens to Paul and attempts to explain him accurately. His writing is clear and passionate. And he is intellectually honest, willing to admit when he does not know something and telling readers when he personally disagrees with Paul on some issue.

How should students think about this book? If they are looking for a basic introduction to the new perspective on Paul, this may not be the first book to read. N. T. Wright's *What St. Paul Really Said* is shorter and more accessible. If they are looking to dig deeper into the most important contributions of E. P. Sanders, this may not be the right book either. His most influential books on Paul will likely continue to be *Paul and Palestinian Judaism* and *Paul, the Law, and the Jewish People*. However, if they are looking for a basic introduction to Paul's letters and thought, this would be a very helpful book. Sanders makes it clear from the beginning of the book that he writes as a historian, not as a theologian (pp. xxxiv-v). Sometimes his theology does peak through, which is basically a liberal Protestant perspective. But for the most part he follows his claim to stick with history, making this book a treasure trove of historical information about Paul's life and letters.

Kevin McFadden
Cairn University, Langhorne, PA

**Hartenstein, Friedhelm, and Konrad Schmid, eds.** *Abschied von der Priesterschrift? Zum Stand der Pentateuchdebatte.* **Veröffentlichungen der Wissenschaftlichen Gesellschaft für Theologie 40. Leipzig: Evangelische Verlagsanstalt, 2015. pp. 218. €38, paperback.**

The collapse of the Documentary Hypothesis beginning in the 1970s left many of the traditional results of critical Pentateuchal research in its wake. Despite the renunciation of the existence of the Yahwist and Elohist sources by Rolf Rendtorff and others, the Priestly Writing (P) has survived largely unscathed, although its characterization as a source is no longer taken for granted. A litany of questions now revolves around the nature of P as a source or redactional layer as well as P's extent and internal stratification. A group of continental scholars gathered to address these and related issues in the Old Testament section of the Wissenschaftlichen Gesellschaft für Theologie in May 2012 at Stuttgart-Hohenheim.

Christoph Levin surveys the history of research on the nature of P and its composition, particularly within the framework of documentary, fragmentary, and supplementary models. Levin finds persuasive the arguments in favor of P's literary independence and attributes the emergence of a separate Priestly history parallel to the Yahwistic/non-P history to the uniqueness of the Priestly worldview, particularly regarding the revelation of God's name and offering sacrifices. For Erhard Blum, the patriarchal traditions of Genesis reveal a varied profile of the Priestly texts. Narrative gaps and the presupposing of pre-P traditions and literary contexts suggest that P is a redaction, but coherent narrative threads provide evidence for an originally independent source. To account for both types of evidence, Blum proposes a multi-staged process for P's composition: Priestly tradents composed drafts of P that aimed toward combination with the non-P traditions from the outset. At a secondary stage, the Priestly tradents combined their P drafts with the non-P materials. In this way, the Priestly tradents function as both the authors and redactors of P. Jan Christian Gertz's examination of Gen 5 argues that the Priestly texts in Gen 1–11 originally constituted an independent source. Gertz counters several common arguments that suggest P is a redactional layer with traditional literary-critical observations. Most uniquely, Gertz proposes that SamP Gen 5, which he considers older than the MT and LXX versions, forms a non-narrative introduction to P's Flood story and prepares the way for the statement of worldwide corruption in 6:11–13. The first five individuals listed in the genealogy establish a life expectancy of around 900 years. The second five individuals, excluding Enoch and Noah due to their close relationships with God, suggest an inverse relationship: increased worldwide sin results in a decrease in length of life. Christoph Berner considers the Priestly texts in Exod 1–14 a redactional supplement to the pre-P texts, but the overall redactional history of the Exodus narratives is significantly more complicated. Berner detects four major editorial layers: (1) a pre-P layer that is much smaller than traditionally assumed; (2) a Priestly expansion of the pre-P texts (=$P^1$, which is basically the same as the traditional Priestly *Grundschrift* [$P^g$] or "basic layer"); (3) substantial post-P additions that are part of a broader late-Deuteronomistic Hexateuchal redaction; and (4) a secondary Priestly layer (=$P^2$) that corresponds to Reinhard Achenbach's "theocratic revision" in the book of Numbers. Thomas Römer considers the same texts as Berner, but arrives at different results. The P texts in Exod 6; 7–9; and 14 originally constituted a continuous and independent narrative thread. Doublets (e.g., Exod 3//Exod 6) provide the most persuasive evidence for originally independent sources, since supplementary models expect a Priestly redaction of pre-P traditions to produce a less fractured narrative. Römer recognizes the absence of an introduction for Moses in P, which is problematic for source models but finds it more compelling to believe that the Priestly tradents assumed familiarity with the Moses traditions or that parts of the Priestly thread were omitted when they were worked into the Pentateuchal narrative than it is to believe that supplementary models would produce doublets. Eckart Otto investigates the relationship between post-exilic *Fortschreibungen* in Leviticus and Deuteronomy. Although Lev 17–26 receives and adapts the Deuteronomic Code, Deut 11:13-17 evinces reception of Lev 26. Deut 11:13-17 contains lexemes otherwise unique to Lev 26 and raises questions about circumcision of the heart that only find their answer in Deut 11. Also, whereas Yhwh speaks in first person in Lev 26, Moses takes on Yhwh's words in first person in Deut 11:13-15 rather than in a third person report of Yhwh's speech. Despite the grammatical awkwardness, Moses's adoption of the first person speech is purposeful: it betrays dependence upon Lev 26 and functions as a bridge to Deut 28 by highlighting Moses's role as prophetic interpreter of Torah. Christophe Nihan explores Pentateuchal models of composition and stratification through the lens of Lev 26. He concludes that Lev 26's concept of covenant presupposes the integration of P and non-P materials in Genesis and Exodus. The author who inserted Lev 17–26 into its present location has a much more limited role than previously thought. He is not the redactor of the entire Pentateuch or associated with a Holiness School. Instead, this author's work coincides with the emergence and redaction of Leviticus as an individual book (scroll). By the time of the insertion of Lev 27, a major break between the scrolls of Leviticus and Numbers had been firmly established.

The present volume's title bears obvious formal similarities to the 2002 collection of essays entitled *Abschied vom Jahwist* (and the English edition *Farewell to the Yahwist?*, SBL, 2006), but the contributors do not bid adieu to the Priestly Writing in the same way that scholars have increasingly rejected the traditional conception of a Yahwist. They maintain that the Priestly Writing (along with Deuteronomy) still comprises the cornerstone of critical research, but the proliferation of models to explain the literary character of the Priestly texts highlights many exegetical disagreements. The contributors' work represents the triumph of tradition-historical criticism at least in the sense that the literary character of P must be evaluated in a sort of piecemeal fashion. So for instance, the source character of Gen 1–11 cannot be extrapolated and applied to the ancestral traditions. Each block of tradition must first be evaluated on its own, and only after all the relevant texts have been examined can a broader synthesis be pursued. All contributors incorporate a range of critical methodologies in their studies, but redaction criticism is generally given pride of place. The essays by Gertz and Otto highlight the increasing importance of text-critical studies for literary criticism. Nihan's association of Lev 26 with the redaction of the book of Leviticus is provocative and potentially raises similar questions about the redaction of Genesis and Exodus as books, although Leviticus may be uniquely situated for such questions due to its thoroughly Priestly character.

My most significant reservation is the tendency to assign an increasing number of texts to post-Priestly strata. David Carr in particular has pointed out that the criterion of the coordination/harmonization of Priestly and non-Priestly language on its own is insufficient to assign texts to post-Priestly strata. According to Carr, scribes employed processes of coordination and harmonization both before and after the combination of the Priestly and non-Priestly materials. Such observations suggest that the distribution of Priestly and non-Priestly materials is not nearly as neat and even as might be expected. Simply because a given text contains both Priestly and non-Priestly terms or concepts does not necessarily mean that such coordination/harmonization only emerges in post-Priestly layers of the Pentateuch/Hexateuch. That said, Otto's article, which posits arguments for direction of dependence in post-Priestly layers of Leviticus and Deuteronomy, exemplifies plausible ways forward.

For (especially non-German-speaking) students of biblical studies, *Abschied von der Priesterschrift?* contributes much more than simply a look at present continental studies of the Priestly strata of the Pentateuch. Levin's concise but thorough review of research is a useful entry point into current scholarship on P. Because the articles by Berner and Römer analyze the same texts, they serve as a particularly helpful way to compare how different scholars prioritize different types of evidence and methodological approaches in order to arrive at workable results. Without prior introduction to critical studies of the Pentateuch, the various labels for different Priestly strata (the more traditional $P^g$, $P^s$, H; Blum's KP; Berner's $P^1$, $P^2$; etc.) might be confusing. Introductions to Pentateuchal studies like those by Jean-Louis Ska (*Introduction to Reading the Pentateuch*, Eisenbrauns, 2006) and Joseph Blenkinsopp (*The Pentateuch*, Yale University Press, 2000) will be particularly helpful for filling such introductory gaps.

Wesley Crouser<br>
Asbury Theological Seminary, Willmore, KY

**Kuruvilla, Abraham.** *A Vision for Preaching: Understanding the Heart of Pastoral Ministry.* **Grand Rapids, MI: Baker Academic, 2015, pp 224, $21.99, softcover.**

Abraham Kuruvilla (MD, University of Kerala; PhD, Baylor College of Medicine; PhD, University of Aberdeen) is research professor of pastoral ministries at Dallas Theological Seminary. He is also a dermatologist in private practice. As the consummate skin doctor, Kuruvilla treats abnormalities of the epidermis in a clinical setting and academically reflects upon divine words transcribed on vellum scrolls. His academic emphasis centers on the intersection of hermeneutics and homiletics for faithful expository preaching. This intersection is explored in his latest book, *A Vision for Preaching*.

Kuruvilla's hermeneutical and homiletical proposal is encapsulated in his vision statement. He says, "Biblical preaching, by a leader of the church, in a gathering of Christians for worship, is the communication of the thrust of a pericope of Scripture discerned by theological exegesis, and of its application to that specific body of believers, that they may be conformed to the image of Christ, for the glory of God—all in the power of the Holy Spirit" (p.1). This vision forms the chapter divisions of Kuruvilla's book and casts a theological vision chapter by chapter for each respective component of his preaching manifesto. He also concludes each chapter with an exegetical "reflection" which are "intended not only to stimulate thought, but also to serve as illustrations of the hermeneutic proposed" (p.26 n.41).

While Kuruvilla attempts to cast a foundational vision for preaching, his most significant contribution to homiletics entails an examination "of how a particular text chosen for preaching dictates specific life change in the lives of Christians" (p.6). In Kuruvilla's assessment, the preacher must go beyond merely applying biblical propositions. He argues that faithful expository preaching must apply the specific theological point of the preaching passage, which he labels a "pericope" (p.19 n.14). Each pericope entails a precise pericopal theology, which should drive every aspect of application (pp.96-99). In this scheme, Kuruvilla opposes principlizing the propositions of the pericope to draw out generalized and varied applications (pp.7-9). Alternatively, he asserts that preachers must apply the specific thrust of the propositions. This exact thrust is dictated by authorial intent and casts a "*world in front of the text*," a world that the hearers are called to "inhabit" (pp.96-97). Thus, "the goal of preaching is . . . to align God's people with God's will in Scripture, pericope by pericope, week by week, sermon by sermon, effecting covenant renewal" (p.133).

In many ways, Kuruvilla's paradigm of pericopal theology is groundbreaking for the discipline of homiletics. Far too often, homileticians have avoided significant discussion of hermeneutical issues. Kuruvilla believes that this neglect often leads to a default "hermeneutic of excavation—the exegetical turning over of tons of earth . . . most of it unfortunately not of any particular use for one seeking to preach a relevant message from a specific text" (p.7). To make sense of this raw data for the preaching event, many preachers resort to "distillation" (p.7). Here, the preacher "performs a distillation of the text into propositions of the sermon that are preached in formulaic fashion, with outlines, points, proofs, and arguments, and with application drawn seemingly at random somewhere along the way. . . . Thus, the dross of texts is distilled off to leave behind the precious residue of theological propositions that is then preached" (p.8).

The obvious hermeneutical problem with this scenario is that a text means something specific, and this specificity must be exposited and applied for faithful proclamation. While principlization and synthesis are valid hermeneutical moves for the discipline of systematic theology, the purpose and function of expository preaching and systematic theology are quite different. The latter is primarily meant to intellectually develop one's theological foundation, whereas the former is meant to transform one's intellect, emotions, and will with pericopal theology. Because each pericope calls for specific covenantal obedience, the expository preacher is not free to principlize a pericope because he would simultaneously be generalizing the pericope's application. Since generalized applications are seen as lacking practicality, the preacher, in the name of relevance, is tempted to emphasize his own specific application which he extrapolates from the general principle. In this move from generalization to specificity, it is unlikely that the preacher's application matches the pericope's specific applicatory demands. Kuruvilla's hermeneutical solution to this problem is for "the preacher [to] . . . pay close attention to the text, not just to what is being said, but also to how it is being said and why, in order that the agenda of the author—that is, the thrust of the text, the theology of the pericope—may be discerned" (p.106). Kuruvilla is right to see that the key to faithful preaching is to re-present the pericope in its fullness.

Whereas Kuruvilla's hermeneutic excels at the level of the pericope, he fails to see the role of redemptive-history for preaching (pp.98-99). Here, Kuruvilla neglects the sanctifying gospel in applying pericopal theology to Christians during the sermon. In its place, he proposes a concept he calls "Christiconic interpretation" (p.138). By this, he means that embracing the specific demands of pericopal theology conforms one to the corresponding attributes of the image of Christ (p.138). It appears that Kuruvilla has coined an empty phrase so that he can argue his model "[preaches] Christ" (p.140). This is seen in the fact that if one eliminates the Christiconic component from Kuruvilla's vision, it is functionally the same concept, and reveals that Kuruvilla's model does not actually lead one to preach Christ. This is a troublesome omission.

*A Vision for Preaching* is Kuruvilla's third book on the homiletical and hermeneutical intersection of pericopal theology. It stands as a refined and much more accessible homiletic in comparison to his other two offerings (*Text to Praxis: Hermeneutics and Homiletics in Dialogue*, Boomsbury T&T Clark, 2009; *Privilege the Text! A Theological Hermeneutic for Preaching*, Moody, 2013). While the advanced student may want to engage *Privilege the Text!*, followed by *Text to Praxis*, all students should begin with *A Vision for Preaching*. This book uniquely gives students and pastors a strong theoretical and practical understanding of expository preaching that faithfully re-presents a biblical text and applies the text's precise application. The importance of this book for the student and pastor is found in the reality that it is fairly easy to preach biblical truth from the pulpit when one is grounded in sound doctrine, but it is far more difficult to faithfully exposit a biblical text so that its peculiarities are seen and sensed by the congregation. *A Vision for Preaching* will also dissolve the mistaken notion that a preacher is faithful to his task simply because he preaches biblical truth and makes it clear and practical for the congregation. Preachers need a deeper sense of what faithful exposition entails, and Kuruvilla's vision provides the necessary clarity to achieve expository faithfulness. At the same time, because Kuruvilla's hermeneutic is incomplete, the student should also be acquainted with the role of biblical theology for preaching. For a good introduction on this topic, see Graeme Goldsworthy, *Preaching the Whole Bible as Christian Scripture: The Application of Biblical Theology to Expository Preaching* (Eerdmans, 2000).

Si Cochran
Southern Hills Baptist Church, Sioux City, IA
Midwestern Baptist Theological Seminary

# BOOK REVIEWS

**Porter, Stanley E. and Andrew W. Pitts.** *Fundamentals of New Testament Textual Criticism.* **Grand Rapids, MI: Eerdmans, 2015, pp. xvi + 202, $22, paperback.**

Stanley Porter and Andrew Pitts have written a new introduction to the subject of New Testament textual criticism that aims to be a "distinctly midlevel textbook" for people who have at least a basic working knowledge of New Testament Greek. The authors note the current lack of such an intermediate work on the subject. Metzger's classic work *The Text of New Testament* (Oxford, 2005) provides a scholarly treatment of textual criticism some of which is too detailed to be useful to seminary students. On the other hand, introductory works, such as Greenlee's *Introduction to New Testament Textual Criticism* (Baker, 1993), while they are suitable for college and first-year seminary students, do not cover some subjects or do not provide the kind of detail that students with more than one year of Koine Greek will find useful for applying text critical principles to the New Testament.

In large part, the authors have succeeded in meeting their goal of an intermediate textbook. The book's aim of being useful to seminary students is enhanced by its covering subjects not directly under the purview of textual criticism. One example is a chapter on the formation of the canon. This is not strictly a concern of text critics, but it is a subject of interest to students as they engage in serious study of the Greek New Testament. Another chapter covers the history of the English Bible and translation theory as it relates to modern English translations. As a third example, in a chapter on types of writing materials, the authors provide a section on literacy and the function of books in the ancient world. These side discussions could prove useful for seminary students, although they are not subjects of text criticism proper.

The book begins with a chapter on basic terminology and concepts. Then, after the abovementioned chapter on the formation of the canon, it proceeds to cover topics that are standard for any book on textual criticism, including chapters on (1) writing materials, paleography, and scribal practices, (2) major New Testament witnesses, (3) text types (or families), and (4) basic concepts of textual variants. Although these topics are also found in more elementary books on textual criticism, Porter and Pitts often provide more detail. An example is in the chapter on major witnesses to the text of the New Testament, where tables are provided with details of papyrus manuscripts, majuscules, and minuscules, respectively. They are helpfully sorted by date, which provides a good running overview to the reader who is not yet familiar with the manuscripts.

The book then provides four chapters on the method of textual criticism. Chapter 7 addresses the major text-critical methodologies, including the stemmatic, the Byzantine / Majority Text, eclectic, and single-text approaches. While criticizing a "thoroughgoing eclecticism," which relies heavily on subjective assessments of internal criteria, the authors advocate a "reasoned eclecticism" that attempts to balance external and internal considerations, with external considerations often being given more weight. The authors conclude that a general consensus exists that this approach alone "can provide adequate objectivity for textual determinations" (p. 96). The authors do admit that reasoned eclecticism has the drawback that clear criteria do not exist for weighing evidence, for example deciding between manuscripts. A little more detail here would be helpful, for example by providing examples of the approach or approaches utilized by either of the modern critical editions – Nestle-Aland (NA27 and NA28) or the United Bible Society (UBS 4 and UBS5) – and how their committees dealt with conflicting manuscript evidence. This would be particularly helpful since the authors indicate that the Nestle-Aland and United Bible Societies editions tend to emphasize the Alexandrian text (p.95).

Chapter 8 covers the analysis of external evidence and argues for the priority of external evidence in making text-critical decisions. The chapter covers external criteria, including date and text type, geographical distribution, and genealogical relationship. The authors highlight a combined set of external criteria that consider (1) the earliest manuscripts, (2) the widest geographical spread, and (3) a lack of genealogical relationship among manuscripts (p.108).

Chapters 9 and 10 are devoted to evaluating and weighing internal evidence. The authors note that internal criteria are important when external evidence is not conclusive. Chapter 9 covers transcriptional probabilities. It begins by stating the fundamental axiom of text criticism known as *the genetic principle*, that the reading that best explains the other variants is probably original. It then covers the traditional canons of text criticism used to determine transcriptional probabilities: (1) scribal errors, (2) difficult readings, (3) shorter and longer readings, (4) less harmonized readings, (5) less grammatically refined readings, and (5) doctrinal alterations. In the final section of the chapter, they address the issue of doctrinal alterations in some detail. They interact with and challenge Bart Ehrman's contention, in his book *Misquoting Jesus*, that scribes routinely changed their received text for doctrinal purposes. The authors conclude, *contra* Ehrman, that doctrinal alteration was rarely a factor in scribal changes, and that it is relatively less important than other criteria for reconstructing the New Testament text.

Chapter 10 looks at another fact of internal evidence: intrinsic possibilities. The factors that are considered are style, cohesion, theological and literary coherence, and linguistic conformity. Regarding style, the principle presented deals with stylistic continuity: "All other things being equal, the variant that shows the most stylistic continuity with the author's style is most likely original" (p. 130). The authors admit up front that the word "style" is not generally defined with any precision. The authors attempt to provide more a objective basis for evaluating style by considering (1) cohesion with the immediate context, (2) coherence with the author's theological emphases, (3) linguistic consistency and (4) the author's use of sources.

The textual factor of cohesion is treated in some detail. The author's define cohesion in terms of what enables texts to "hang together" as a unity, and involves the evaluation of syntax and vocabulary. They go on to note that "any device or form can be used to create a cohesive pattern, and often this will aid in textual criticism." As an example, the authors examine the long ending of Mark and show how the lack of cohesion in vocabulary provides text-critical evidence that it is not original.

Another example from Colossian 3:9 is less convincing, and highlights the somewhat subjective nature of assessing "style" for making text-critical assessments. The authors note that the structure of the section from Colossians 3:5 to 3:12 involves 3 imperatives (in 3:5, 3:8, and 3:12) where in 2 cases (verses 5 and 12) the imperative is followed by a set of indicatives in secondary clauses. The imperative in verse 8, however, does not follow this pattern because according to the critical editions (both NA 27/28 and UBS 4/5), verse 9 also has an imperative and this breaks the pattern proposed for the other 2 imperatives.

The authors note the evidence of one manuscript, P[46], which has a one letter difference (a Greek *eta* instead of *epsilon*) that creates a subjunctive instead of an imperative. They propose that this would be closer to the pattern seen after the other imperatives in verses 5 and 12. They argue that based on the Paul's style, as indicated by the structure they identify, the subjunctive is the more likely reading in verse 9.

To evaluate this claim, one needs to turn to the author's explanation earlier in the chapter of when stylistic considerations might be useful for text criticism, which rightly begins with, "All other things being equal…" That is, when other text-critical factors with a higher priority are not at least moderately conclusive, then issues of style may be considered. In this case, however, external evidence supports the critical editions.

Assuming the external evidence is less than moderately compelling, one could appeal to the internal category of transcriptional probabilities. The change from Greek *epsilon* to *eta* or vice versa cannot be attributed to a straightforward example of itacism (the confusion of letters that were pronounced alike). But the P[46] variant could still be a scribal copying error. If we first assume that the subjunctive of P[46] was original, one might propose how a scribe would change this unusual form to a more expected imperative through changing one letter. But one could also argue the other way. If the style is clearly discernible, why could not the P[46] scribe have changed an imperative to a subjunctive to conform to Paul's stylistic pattern? Here the evidence is not conclusive.

Continuing with a consideration of the internal category of style in this case, the authors propose that one prohibition was substituted for another in verse 9 – that is, a scribe substituted a negated imperative for an original negated subjunctive. But the structure they identify for the passage as a whole is imperative followed by indicatives (that presumably provide explanation). They do not explain why an imperative command in verse 8 followed by a subjunctive command in verse 9 is closer to this pattern.

In addition, in order to make a case based on structural cohesion, one would have to demonstrate from Paul's writings that he tends to set up and then follow such structures consistently, and that content – for example, emphasis or repetition – could not contribute to deviating from a pattern.

In summary, the author's conclusion in this case is not warranted by the evidence. Thus, although considerations of stylistic continuity can be helpful in making text critical judgments, as shown by examining the vocabulary of the long ending of Mark, a different example than the one presented from Colossians would be more helpful.

Chapter 11 deals with modern critical editions of the New Testament and provides a useful primer for Greek students who are interested not only in the history of Greek editions but in the philosophy behind the latest Nestle-Aland (NA) and United Bible Society (UBS) critical editions.

The final chapters treat topics that are useful for seminary students although outside of the discipline of textual criticism. Chapters 12 provides a helpful guide to the critical apparatuses of both the NA and UBS editions of the New Testament. And chapter 13 discusses the history of the English Bible and gives an introduction to translation theory, both topics of interest to Greek students as they learn how not only how to use their Greek New Testaments but how to teach those who do not know Greek.

In summary, Porter and Pitts have provided a good intermediate treatment of textual criticism and some related subjects. The text normally provides good examples that illustrate the principles being presented. This book should prove useful for second-year Greek students. For those looking for more detail, Metzger's book is the standard reference work.

Andy McClurg
Grand Canyon University, Phoenix, AZ

**Rolnick, Philip.** *Origins: God, Evolution, and the Question of the Cosmos.* **Waco: Baylor University Press, 2015, pp.vii + 252, $39.95, hardback.**

Philip Rolnick serves as Professor of Theology at the University of St. Thomas in St. Paul, Minnesota as well as Chair of the Science and Theology Network in the Twin Cities. In addition to *Origins*, Rolnick has authored and edited several books, such as *Person, Grace, and God* (Eerdmans, 2007), *Analogical Possibilities: How Words Refer to God* (Oxford, 1993), *Reflections on Grace* (Cascade Books, 2007), and *Explorations in Ethics: Readings from Across the Curriculum* (Greensboro College Press, 1998). Rolnick has also written numerous chapters in books, articles, and book reviews whose topics range from evolution and theology to anthropology. *Origins* is a helpful book for any student of the Bible who seeks to understand the current debate between evolution and theology.

Rolnick approaches *Origins* with the view that "science and religious faith are not only compatible, but even mutually illuminating" (p.4); they are "partners in the search for truth" (p.5). When it comes to the origin of the universe, "divine creativity and reason are unquestionably present and scientifically discoverable" (p.6). Thus, for the believer today, learning from scientific discover can strengthen one's faith (p.6). Rolnick sets forth the thesis that evolution—contrary to common belief—is not antithetical to Scripture; rather, evolution is in harmony with Scripture. Part II of *Origins* deals with the so-called challenges of evolution to Christianity and shows how they are actually theological advantages. In Part III, Rolnick provides evidence from scientific discoveries of the universe's beginning and its fine-tuning. Using the Gospel of John as a case study, Rolnick also shows how Christians have the tools to unite faith and science. Finally, Part IV seeks to set the previous chapters into the perspective of the believer's daily life – how the Christian understands oneself and his interaction with nature and God, as well as how "the parallels between science and faith . . . can energize the faith of our time" (p.9).

There are two features about *Origins* that I would like to highlight. First, Rolnick's work is easy to follow considering the amount of scientific jargon and data discussed. While most readers are familiar with the basics of Darwinian evolution, Rolnick is able to express more technical issues in a way that non-specialists can easily comprehend. Further, the sheer amount of scientific discoveries discussed—and the varied sub-disciplines of science they cover—illustrate the fact that Rolnick is well-versed in modern science. For instance, Rolnick's chapters on the origin of an inhabitable universe and the finely-tuned nature of the universe present complex ideas from astronomy and astrophysics. The depth at which Rolnick interacts with current scientific discoveries serves to demonstrate that science can support key Christian beliefs regarding the origin of the universe.

The second feature worth commending is Rolnick's attempt to demonstrate that evolution is not a challenge to theism, particularly the theistic belief in the existence of God. Reminiscent of Alvin Plantinga's approach in *Where the Conflict Really Lies* (Oxford, 2011), Rolnick provides a more narrowly focused line of attack by addressing four traditional challenges of evolution against theism: "evolution and divine design" (p.15); "natural selection and a God of love" (p.25); "struggle, pain, and death and the goodness of creation" (p. 28); and "common ancestry and human uniqueness" (p.31). Rolnick admirably exhibits how each of the four "challenges" actually fit within a theistic view of the world. After exposing evolutionary challenges as theistic advantages, Rolnick can then render scientific discoveries not as anti-theistic fodder, but as key components of a larger theistic picture of the world.

The strength of Rolnick's book—demonstrating the compatibility of evolution and theism—is perhaps its greatest weakness as well. Driving the entire work is Rolnick's belief in Darwinian evolution in its entirety. For Rolnick, "the evidence discovered so well fits the theory of evolution, the theory has become predominant among biologists—and many religious leaders" (pp.14-15). Further, because of the shear amount of evidence supporting evolution, "denying the evidence is a poor and counterproductive way of defending the faith" (p.15). Darwinian evolution, for Rolnick, is a brute fact—a basic belief that undergirds his argumentation and even his interpretation of Scripture. As such, Rolnick allows science to speak for itself regarding evolution *in toto* instead of demonstrating *how* the current picture of evolution is correct.

Such a critique may be lost on some, but it is the opinion of this reviewer that the question of whether evolution *in toto* is accurate or not is a fundamental question. That is, one must first argue how Darwinian evolution as a system is accurate before demonstrating the compatibility between evolution and theism. As is, Rolnick's book begs the question that scientific evidence 1) does support the complete package of evolution, and 2) is itself accurate. Accepting evolution *in toto* involves, in part, the epistemological task of interpreting scientific data and determining *how* one knows whether the data accurately portrays reality. Failing to address the epistemological underpinnings of his argument reduces the force of Rolnick's *Origins* to a catalogue of compatible tenets of evolution and theism.

Finally, presenting Darwinian evolution as brute fact leads Rolnick to interpret Scripture through evolutionary lenses, leading to seemingly forced interpretations of particular passages. For instance, for Rolnick, the parable of the talents found in Matthew 25:14-30 "parallels and evolutionary setting" where "progress is applauded and rewarded, and standing still is forbidden" (pp.63-64). The servants who were praised "took intelligent risks and responsibly developed their initial endowments…Just as evolution is dynamic, so too is Jesus' kingdom" (p.64). The servant who buried his talent illustrates, "in biological terms…that [he] is selected against; thrown into the outer darkness, his one talent is taken from him and given to the one who has ten" (p.64). There is a sense in which even non-scientific passages in Scripture are reinterpreted in light of evolution—a method that is problematic and dangerous.

Philip Rolnick's *Origins* is a book that deserves attention from any Christian confronted with the relationship between evolution and Christian belief. Despite the weaknesses mentioned above, Rolnick's work has apologetical value for the believer as it transforms key challenges against Christianity into theological advantages. For the believer who does not hold to evolution or only accepts it in part, *Origins* serves to demonstrate the probability of evolution in light of theism. Evolution need not be a defeater for theism. For the believer who does hold to evolution, *Origins* serves as a resource that tears down the wall between evolution and theism. Regardless of where one stands regarding evolution, Rolnick's book is a good starting point into the discussion on evolution and theism. A comparable book is Karl Giberson's *Saving Darwin: How to Be a Christian and Believe in Evolution* (HarperCollins, 2008). Similarly, William Dembski's *Intelligent Design: The Bridge Between Science and Theology* (InterVarsity, 1999), like Rolnick, seeks to demonstrate the compatibility between science and theology, but it does so from the perspective of Intelligent Design. Finally, Michael Behe's *Darwin's Black Box: The Biochemical Challenge to Evolution* (Touchstone, 1996) challenges evolution from the argument of fine-tuning. These helpful books provide the scope of the debate within Christian circles regarding the relationship (if any) between evolution and theism.

J. Daniel McDonald<br>
Boyce College<br>
Liberty University Online

**Vanhoozer, Kevin, and Owen Strachan, *The Pastor as Public Theologian: Reclaiming a Lost Vision*, Grand Rapids, MI: Baker Academic, 2015, pp. 240, $19.99, hardback.**

Kevin Vanhoozer (PhD, University of Cambridge) is research professor of systematic theology at Trinity Evangelical Divinity School. An ordained elder, he has written or edited sixteen books. Owen Strachan (PhD, Trinity Evangelical Divinity School) is associate professor of Christian theology and director of The Center for Theological and Cultural Engagement at Midwestern Baptist Theological Seminary. Also, Strachan is the author of six books, and he is the president of the Council on Biblical Manhood and Womanhood. In addition to Vanhoozer and Strachan, pastoral contributions are woven throughout the work from twelve ministers across American and European evangelical contexts.

Vanhoozer, Strachan, and a team of seasoned practitioners provide a sweeping rebuttal to the contemporary approach of pastoral ministry. Throughout this work, readers are confronted with a passionate plea to recover a historical and biblical view that pastoral ministry is first and foremost a theological calling. The authors dispel the mentality that pastoral ministry is one of *only* praxis and robust theological reflection is reserved *only* for the academy. The authors argue that "theological minds belong in ecclesial bodies. We don't wish to exaggerate: there is a place for academic theology, but it is *second* place. First place – pride of theological place – belongs to the pastor theologian" (p.xi, emphasis in original). The pastor theologian is not the only type of theologian, but his office is one of public *visibility* and ecclesial *necessity*.

Vanhoozer introduces the book with a riveting analysis of public, ecclesial theology. He traces historical and practical causes to establish his premise that pastors have lost their theological vision for ministry. Similarly and perhaps consequently, churches have lost their vision of a theologically robust pastoral office in favor of modern leadership and management skills gleaned from secular business practices. In order to reclaim a biblical vision, Vanhoozer wisely describes how the pastoral office is public and theological, and he provides the groundwork for prescribing a biblical and theological solution.

For Vanhoozer, a pastor is a public theologian because he says (through preaching and other ecclesial responsibilities) what God is doing in Christ. Declaring God's work in Christ is the heralding of a theological message designed by God for needy sinners. The pastor equips his congregation with the gospel, and he does so to build up an active body of believers committed to spreading the gospel to all aspects of life. Thus, a pastor is a public theologian because he is involved with people in and for community (pp.16-17).

After the introduction, the book divides neatly into two parts: In part 1, Strachan provides two chapters which focus on biblical and historical theology. Strachan writes with acute awareness of how the pastor theologian model is indeed reflected within biblical and historical theology. Thus, this book is not advocating a new paradigm for ministry but a recovery of one rooted in sound biblical practice and unquestionably evidenced through historical reflection. Strachan's chapter on biblical theology is superb. He carefully details the connections between the tri-fold office of Jesus (the *munus triplex*) as prophet, priest, and king and connecting them to pastoral theology. Strachan argues that ministers of the new covenant serve as priests by ministering grace, serve as kings by ministering wisdom, and serve as prophets by ministering truth. These ministries are emphatically theological, and they are the work of an ecclesial, public theologian. Seminary students will learn much from Strachan in this section, and seasoned pastors, at the very least, will find comforting reassurance or a helpful corrective.

In part 2, Vanhoozer provides two chapters focusing on systematic and practical theology. Readers accustomed to Vanhoozer's previous books will recognize these chapters as reflective of his other writings. Vanhoozer's writing is creative and probing, and throughout his work, he answers questions the reader does not even realize were asked. His chapter on systematic theology is historical in reflection and instructive in application. Readers are forced to consider the moods of theology (indicative and imperative). Pastoral ministry focuses on teaching the indicatives of theology, and the goal of this teaching is to "indicate *what is in Christ*" (p.110, emphasis in original). Ministers address the indicative mood through biblical literacy and a biblically informed understanding of cultural literacy. Ministers also employ the imperative mood by declaring how one is to live and pursue human flourishing in light of what is offered to believers in Christ. Throughout this chapter on practical theology, Vanhoozer refers to ministers as artisans in the house of God. As an artisan, the minister work as an Evangelist, Catechist, Liturgist, and Apologist. The twelve pastoral contributions are inserted within both parts and provide helpful reflections on the lengthier chapters. As academic theologians, one may be critical that these scholars are writing a corrective of pastor theologians. This criticism, however, loses any traction when readers grasp the helpful and wide ranging subjects the twelve pastors include in this work.

Finally, the book concludes with Vanhoozer's fifty-five theses on the pastor as public theologian. Most of these thoughts are covered in one way or another in the book, but a few notable entries are worth further reflection. For example, thesis forty-eight focuses on the role of the sermon in assisting the congregation in interpreting culture. This thesis, and others, deserves further reflection, but each of them are descriptive enough that individual readers can apply them to their own contexts. While the book does not deal with the qualifications listed in 1 Timothy 3, the overall emphasis of the book does provide some substance to the qualification Paul establishes that elders should be apt to teach.

Students preparing for ministry should incorporate this book into their theological training. The authors present a compelling case rooted in various theological disciplines. Regardless of which contributor one reads, a consistent love for the church exists throughout this work, and students need to learn from this approach. The correctives listed advance needed conversations without being pushy or insensitive. Students in preparation for ministry can save themselves a lot of heartache by following the direction the book offers for ministry vision. Ultimately, pastoral ministry built upon shallow platitudes and cutting edge marketing skills are nothing more than a house of cards. And when those houses crash, many ministers do not recover. Capturing a vision of pastoral ministry embracing the role of public theologian sets a course of growth and strength for ministers and the churches they serve. In addition to this fine work, students interested in reading more widely on this subject are encouraged to read *The Pastor Theologian: Resurrecting an Ancient Vision* by Gerald Hiestand and Todd Wilson. Both Hiestand and Wilson are contributors to the work under review, and their own volume on this subject addresses additional subject matter worthy of investigation.

Throughout this work, Vanhoozer, Strachan, and their team of twelve contributors have helped shape a necessary conversation within the academy and church. The authors did not ask every question within this crucial conversation, nor did they cultivate consistently explicit examples of how to be a pastor theologian. But these observations do not hinder the helpful instruction and application within this book. My prayer is that current and future pastors will use this work and others as way to bolster the pastoral office to its theological position. May the Lord use this work to help in the reformation of pastoral calling, and may future pastors resolve to embrace their theological role as public, ecclesial theologians for the glory of Christ and His church.

Justin L. McLendon
Grand Canyon University, Phoenix, AZ

**Duguid, Iain M. *The Song of Songs*. Westmont, IL: IVP Academic, 2015, pp. 160, $15, paperback.**

Iain Duguid (PhD, University of Cambridge) is professor of religion and Old Testament at Grove City College in Pennsylvania. Duguid has written several works including *Hero of Heroes: Seeing Christ in the Beatitudes* (P&R Publishing, 2001) and *Ezekiel and the Leaders of Israel* (Brill, 1994). He has also contributed volumes to several commentary series including the *Reformed Expository Commentary* (Daniel, Esther & Ruth), the *NIV Application Commentary* (Ezekiel), and *Preaching the Word* (Numbers). *Song of Songs* is a work that will benefit both student and pastor in their study of Solomon's love poem.

Duguid wrote *Song of Songs* based on "a conviction that it [Song of Songs] was not generally being preached adequately (or at all) in the evangelical or Reformed circles in which I move" (p.9). The book sets out to provide a comprehensive commentary on the text to alleviate this perceived shortcoming. This is accomplished methodically by examining questions of authorship and date, themes and structures, and concluding with an analysis of the text itself.

Duguid's work shines in two areas. First, his sensitivity to the hermeneutical issues and tendencies at play is excellent. Duguid surveys various attempts to categorize and classify the Song. These interpretations include: love song, allegory, natural, typological, and more. In this he rightly worries that "the desire for relevant application of the biblical text can make allegorists of us all" (p.31). He contends, however, that it is just as problematic for a text to exist without connection to the present. Therefore, he rightly argues for a balanced approach in understanding the text. Duguid sees the Song as it is most naturally presented, that is, as a work of wisdom from the ancient Near East speaking about marriage. This foundation is augmented by a realization that a study of human relations can have theological implications. "To put it in more explicit biblical terms, our broken human relationships tell us something about our broken relationship with God" (p.38). Duguid's interpretative lens is impressive as it allows him to remain grounded in the history and culture of the text while remaining sensitive to the metanarrative themes of Scripture itself. It is clear that Duguid seeks to be as faithful as he can to the original intent of the book.

The second excellent feature of the book is in its relevance to the modern reader. With Western, especially American, culture's preoccupation with sex and eroticism, Duguid makes a point of showing a biblical counterbalance in viewing sex. He helpfully points out that the Song does highly praise sex and views it as a beautiful gift of God, but also notes that the author of the Song doesn't go out of his way to be crass (p.95). Sex is more than a biological action biblically, it is an event in which the whole person becomes 'one', in the Genesis sense, with their partner. Students and pastors alike will find great practical application in Duguid's words on this matter.

The only critique I would venture for Duguid's work is that he too lightly engages the history of ancient Near East and its relevance in interpretation. As noted earlier, Duguid believes the work to primarily be interpreted as a piece of wisdom literature of the ancient world. As such, the Song exists in a genre that contains other examples from neighboring cultures. This is mentioned in passing for example when Duguid speaks of Egyptian love literature (p.95). Rarely though does he engage the metaphors, images, and symbols that would be part of the genre of love literature. This omission may be due to the pastoral focus of the work, or perhaps a concern that such inclusions would push the required knowledge on the reader's part beyond a basic level. In either case the shortcoming remains. There does seem to be a missed opportunity to both advance scholarship and enrich readers in this area.

Throughout *Song of Songs* the reader is pushed to know, meditate upon, and apply biblical wisdom in regards to marriage. Duguid has written an excellent commentary that calls one to draw closer to God. This work is a welcome addition for students seeking to get an introductory view of the Song of Songs, and it will be an excellent addition to any pastor's library. In light of rising rates of divorce and a generally cavalier attitude towards sex permeating our churches, Duguid brings godly truth and offers practical applications from the Bible that can mend the broken hearted.

The Tyndale Old Testament Commentary series seeks to help readers understand the Bible as Scripture and to be able to approach it without being lost in the technical debates of academia. On that count Duguid's work is a resounding success. Students should not rely though on this as their only source for more academically focused work. Those that would wish a more serious lexical approach should consider turning to Longman's *Song of Songs* (Eerdmans, 2001) or Garrett's *Song of Songs, Lamentations* (Nelson, 2004). For more historic and cultural insight into the Song, students should consider Othmar Keel's *The Song of Songs: A Continental Commentary* (Fortress, 1997).

Brian Koning
Midwestern Baptist Theological Seminary, Kansas City, MO

**Al Fasol, *A Complete Guide to Sermon Delivery*. Nashville, TN: Broadman & Holman Publishers, 1996, pp. 164, $25.89 (paperback).**

Al Fasol, in his book, *A Complete Guide to Sermon Delivery*, offers those that preach a practical guide to effectively preach better and at a higher level of excellence. Fasol bases his work around six core sermon principles, that if understood and practically applied can help any preacher evolve from good to great in his sermon delivery. These six areas of focused study include vocal production, facial expression, eye contact, posture, articulation, and gestures.

In this work, Fasol makes it clear that while sermon delivery has much to do with a preacher's personality, sermon delivery must grow and change as the preacher matures and grows in his walk with God, as well as the preparation and delivery of a sermon. As we understand life and ministry, we see that healthy things grow and growing things change. Fasol in this work clearly lines out why this principle is indeed correct and how the preacher can actually achieve growth in sermon preparation and delivery. By focusing on the aspects of proper vocal production and articulation, the proper and most effective facial expressions, continued eye contact with the audience, presence, posture, and gestures the preacher becomes a very effective preaching instrument to any and all audiences.

There are several positive features to Fasol's work that are worth mentioning. Utilizing the entire body for sermon delivery is probably the most important and practical piece to Fasol's work, as he proposes that actually doing the listed exercises can the preacher train his body to actually communicate more effectively than every thought or imagined. This area is offered with many practical applications for the preacher to work through and on, with the goal of becoming an accomplished and effective communicator.

Another big strength to this work is the way that Fasol encourages the preacher to continually be looking at evaluating how well he is putting these exercises into practice and how much growth the preacher is seeing in his own sermon deliveries. Fasol encourages his readers to approach preaching in a very honest manner, to be open about evaluating where the preacher is weak, for the sake of growing in those areas and focusing on growth as the goal. Fasol assumes that if the preacher can examine his weakness honestly, then he will be better equipped to focus on those areas and actually use those weak areas to highlight the strength areas of preaching. This was a great direction to take the work in, and was very encouraging to read how weakness can be a great motivator in preaching, as this was a concept that this reader never looked at previously.

However his greatest strength is the continual push of wanting to grow better in sermon delivery. Fasol shows how personality driven preaching can actually hinder the message that is being communicated, as a preacher who is "good at preaching" can become complacent and uninterested in actually becoming a master at his preaching craft. This concept really made this reader sit back and look at his past preaching ministries to evaluate how important growth in sermon delivery is and was, while moving forward looking to utilize these areas of focus to become a better communicator, not just in the pulpit but in every aspect of life.

One of the weaknesses of this book is that the author spends a considerable amount of time addressing media relations, specifically how to prepare for radio and television, when he could have spent more focus on the sermon delivery from the pulpit. While there is some value in what Fasol has written in Chapter six, this area could be seen as adding more of an issue in contemporary preaching today.

Radio and television preachers nowadays are everywhere and whole ministries are being committed to radio and television production. Preaching should never be a production of anything, and in today's society there are so many false prophets and teachers, even on "Christian radio and television" that the focus really should be in those areas. Fasol almost gives his thumbs up to radio and television speaking, as if that's the goal of all preachers, to reach that platform as a goal.

Again, there is value in what Fasol has proposed, but from this reader's perspective he is walking a very thin line when he expresses how to approach radio and television, because if this work is truly a complete guide to preaching, then the practical application of chapter six would be to focus on getting on radio and television, which one could argue isn't preaching or sermon delivery at all.

Fasol helps the reader to remember the importance of practice in sermon delivery and how utilizing the concepts put forth in this work are necessary to grow in sermon delivery. Fasol even goes so far as to explain that by utilizing the physical aspects of all the six areas of focus, that preachers will be able to grow in many areas, not just the vocal oration of preaching.

Many feel that preaching is just about what you say, but Fasol explains very clearly that preaching is not just or only about the message and text, but how you communicate that message physically as a whole. Fasol focuses not just on what a preacher says, but how they say it verbally, in every physical way possible, utilizing the whole body to be as effective in sermon delivery as possible.

This work is an extremely valuable resource for all preachers, as it is designed to help those who preach become better and more skilled at the art and craft of preaching. For this reader, the work is something that I am thankful for being exposed to as I look to reengage the next stage of my preaching ministry, as there is so much depth and content in it. Fasol has presented very practical steps for those who want to improve on their preaching and sermon delivery.

Bob C. Greene<br>
Oxford Graduate School, Dayton, TN

**Bodner, Keith.** *After the Invasion: A Reading of Jeremiah 40-44.* **Oxford: Oxford University Press, 2015, pp. viii + 179, $90, hardback.**

Keith Bodner is Professor of Religious Studies at Crandall University in New Brunswick, Canada. Bodner has written several books and commentaries including *Elisha's Profile in the Book of Kings: the Double Agent* (Oxford, 2013), *Jeroboam's Royal Drama* (Oxford, 2012), and *1 Samuel: A Narrative Commentary* (Sheffield Phoenix, 2008), among other titles. Bodner's writings have largely been within the area of narrative criticism. *After the Invasion* is an excellent work that will help any thoughtful student of the Bible understand the text of Jeremiah, and particularly Jeremiah 40-44, better.

*After the Invasion* was written "to make a contribution to the interpretation of Jer 40-44 by undertaking a reading of the text with a primary interest in the narrative poetics of the text" (p. 3). In doing this Bodner examines that text of Jeremiah 40-44 in a sequential manner and focuses on features within the narrative like characterization, geography, point of view, temporal compression, plot, intertextuality, and irony.

There are two features of this book that I would like to highlight. First, it is well-written and well researched. This work combines two things that are rare in academic books. It is well-written and easy to read. The author is exceptionally clear in the points that he is communicating while at the same time being scholarly and advancing scholarship. There are several places where this can be found within the book. One example is near the beginning of the book when Bodner is discussing plot within a story. When doing this he is interacting with academic scholarship (particularly the works of Ricoeur and Doak), but explaining the concepts in a way that the uninitiated will appreciate and understand (see pp.3-5). This work is approachable by anyone who has a basic understanding of the outworking of narrative poetics, but will be most appreciated by those who have a stronger foundation in this area.

The second admirable feature of this work that I would like to highlight is helpfulness of Bodner's methodology and how this leads to a strong reading of the text. One of the places where this is visible is in his discussion of Jeremiah's "double release" in Jeremiah 39:11-14 and 40:1. Many commentators spend excessive time on extremely hypothetical theories. While Bodner understands that there is a place for such theories within biblical scholarship (there are ample footnotes referencing other scholarship in the field showing that Bodner is more than familiar with history of scholarship both in the field of narrative criticism and the book of Jeremiah) he focuses on understanding the text as we have it and how Jeremiah's "double release" functions within the narrative. Bodner supports his interpretation by discussing how plots can rearrange, expand, contract, or even repeat. This provides a much richer reading of the text as it stands. Bodner's interpretation, that the narrator is providing different perspectives for the same event, is an extremely clear and compelling reading of the text. This understanding of the double release then allows each of the scenes to "have their own distinctive thematic emphases" (p.25). Even on the rare occasion where I do disagree with Bodner's reading of the text it is evident that he has wrestled with the text and supported his view.

The only critiques that I would offer are that the organization of the work could be slightly clearer and it would have been helpful for Bodner to frame Jeremiah 40-44 more fully in the narrative space of 34-39. Bodner does draw the reader's attention back to these previous chapters frequently, but the reader should be very familiar with Jeremiah 34-39 before starting this book. It would have also been helpful to the reader if the texts from Jeremiah being covered within the individual chapters would have been clearly marked within the chapter title or subtitle. Bodner does lay these out within the introduction and the texts being covered within each chapter are evident when reading through the book cover to cover (which is how this book is intended to be read, not like a traditional commentary), but for quicker reference and research this feature would have been helpful.

*After the Invasion* is a great example of how a reading of a biblical narrative should be done using narrative poetics. *After the Invasion* would be a great addition to the libraries of students and pastors. It is a great supplementary volume to any major commentary on Jeremiah and should be one of the first resources that is consulted when reading, preaching, or studying Jeremiah 40-44. This book should probably not be a student's first book in the area of narrative poetics, though this book can certainly be read and appreciated without a background in this area of study. This book does provide a prime example to students of what narrative poetics looks like when practiced. Before reading this book a student who is in the beginning stages of learning about narrative would be helped by reading introductory works in the field. I would recommend starting with the chapter on narrative within most standard hermeneutics books. The chapters on narrative in Duvall and Hays's *Grasping God's Word* (Zondervan, 2012), Patterson and Köstenberger's *Invitation to Biblical Interpretation* (Kregel, 2011), and Fee and Stuart's *How to Read the Bible for All Its Worth* (Zondervan, 2014) are good very basic introductions to this field. After grasping the basic content of this study the student will be helped by consulting introductory works focused on narrative poetics like Alter's *The Art of Biblical Narrative* (Basic, 2011), Ryken's *How Bible Stories Work* (Weaver, 2015), or Longman's *Literary Approaches to Biblical Interpretation* (Zondervan, 1987). There are also several advanced works in the field by Amit (*Reading Biblical Narratives*, Fortress, 2001), Berlin (*Poetics and Interpretation of Biblical Narrative*, Eisenbrauns, 1994), Bar-Efrat (*Narrative Art in the Bible*, T&T Clark, 2004), Sternberg (*The Poetics of Biblical Narrative*, Indiana University Press, 1987), and others that the advanced student would greatly benefit from.

Daniel S. Diffey<br>
Grand Canyon University, Phoenix, AZ

# BOOK REVIEW INDEX

*The Flow of the Psalms: Discovering Their Structure and Theology*
by Palmer O. Robertson (Reviewed by Stephen J. Smith).........................................................73

*Paul: The Apostle's Life, Letters, and Thought* by E.P. Sanders
(Reviewed by Kevin McFadden) ............................................................................................75

*Abschied von der Priesterschrift? Zum Stand der Pentateuchdebatte* edited by
Friedhelm Hartenstein and Konrad Schmid (Reviewed by Wesley Crouser).......................79

*A Vision for Preaching: Understanding the Heart of Pastoral Ministry*
by Abraham Kuruvilla (Reviewed by Si Cochran).................................................................82

*Fundamentals of New Testament Textual Criticism*
by Stanley E. Porter and Andrew W. Pitts (Reviewed by Andy McClurg)............................85

*Origins: God, Evolution, and the Question of the Cosmos* by Philip Rolnick
(Reviewed by J. Daniel McDonald)........................................................................................88

*The Pastor as Public Theologian: Reclaiming a Lost Vision*
by Kevin Vanhoozer and Owen Strachan (Reviewed by Justin McLendon)........................91

*The Song of Songs* by Iain Duguid (Reviewed by Brian Koning)................................................94

*A Complete Guide to Sermon Delivery* by Al Fasol (Reviewed by Bob Greene).....................95

*After the Invasion: A Reading of Jeremiah 40-44* (Reviewed by Daniel S. Diffey) ................97

www.ingramcontent.com/pod-product-compliance
Lightning Source LLC
Chambersburg PA
CBHW080406170426
43193CB00016B/2832